Relationship — are you sure you want one?

By Simone Milasas & Brendon Watt

Relationship — are you sure you want one?

ISBN: 978-1-63493-222-6 (trade paperback)
ISBN: 978-1-63493-223-3 (ebook)

For questions, please contact:
Access Consciousness Publishing
406 Present Street
Stafford, TX 77477 USA
accessconsciousnesspublishing.com

'Don't look for what will make you happy. Be happy just for the fun of it.'

Gary Douglas

Foreword

The authors of this book, Simone Milasas and Brendon Watt, are two of the most courageous people I know, who have a relationship that is about creation and continuous contribution to each other and the world around them.

What they are creating and what they talk about in this book are not normal. So if you are looking for another book to tell you what you have been doing wrong and what you need to do to have the perfect relationship, this is not the book for you.

But if you have ever wondered what it would be like to have a relationship with a partner, with your friends, or with yourself that allows you to create more possibilities in every area your life, then this just may be the book that invites you to actually have that.

Brendon and Simone have been willing to look at every aspect of themselves and their relationship and have the vulnerability to share it all with you in this book. I have not seen many relationships that actually work, let alone a relationship that I admire, yet what they are creating is all that and so much more.

I am honoured to be their friend, and I am continuously inspired by what they have shown me is actually possible in a relationship where true caring, gratitude and creation are the leaping-off point to having more. I am greater for it. I am empowered to choose something completely different because of it. And, after reading this book, my bet is that you will be too.

Emily Evans Russell

Table of Contents

Introduction

So many people believe their happiness depends on being in a relationship.

In truth, you don't have to be in a relationship with another person to be happy. You can simply choose to wake up happy every day.

Relationship is not the source for creating your life. You are the source of creation. You are the catalyst of change. You are the one who can create the life you truly desire and you are the one who created your life as it currently is.

If you would like to have a great relationship, whether it is with someone else or with yourself, and haven't been able to create it so far, please don't give up.

What if you made a demand of yourself, and a request of the universe to start making different choices? And, stop judging yourself. No matter where you are right now, things can change.

In the past, we both had relationships that were pretty awful and even abusive in different ways. So, when we first got together, neither of us were willing to be in a relationship that didn't work. We made a commitment to use the tools of Access

Consciousness® every single time we got stuck. It hasn't always been the easiest thing to do. Some of the tools make us really uncomfortable, yet we have used them to create a phenomenal relationship.

For us, relationship is not about security or safety. For us, relationship is about kindness and caring and always empowering the other person to be greater, even if that means they might leave!

A relationship doesn't have to be forever. Every day is a new day. Every day is about, what can we choose today and what can we create together?

We do not say that we have got it right — because we haven't. We have the Access Consciousness tools and we use them to create greater possibilities and greater intimacy every day.

This book is about the pragmatics of relationship and how a relationship can actually work to your advantage. It is written from both our perspectives so you can have a man's point of view and a woman's point of view on being in relationship.

If you are looking for an answer, sorry. There is no answer.

We don't talk a lot about love and romance. We offer many tools and questions you can use every single day. Please know that no matter how grudgingly you use the tools in this book, they will work.

Relationship is not always easy and so we wanted to put everything on the table and talk about all the things that we have been and done: all the joy, all the potency, all the frustration. We are willing to do this as an invitation to people to be true to themselves.

You are one of the brave ones. You opened this book, so take what you can from it and please, have fun with it and enjoy your relationship!

Simone & Brendon

P.S. This book is written in the Queen's English. We are Australian after all!

PART ONE
RELATIONSHIP
DONE DIFFERENT

SIMONE MILASAS & BRENDON WATT

CHAPTER 1

I expected to be single forever

Simone

How many great relationships do you see out there? I don't mean long lasting relationships. I am talking about caring relationships where you empower each other to be as great as you can be — if you are honest, there are not very many like that.

This was something I knew well, since when it came to choosing bad relationships, I was no different from anybody else. In the past I was well known for dating men who would judge me and my body. That energy matched the judgements I had of me. So if these men judged me and my body, then our judgements were the perfect match!

I also wasn't willing to be vulnerable enough to admit that kindness and caring exist on this planet. So for years and years, I refused to have a relationship.

It was easy to justify this decision because looking around, I did not see any great relationships. So why would I choose one?

Somewhere in my universe I expected to be single for the rest of my life.

My desire was to create something that had an impact on the planet and changed the way people perceive and judge each other. Since I loved to travel the world, I thought I would have my own business, as I consider business to be the most fun and creative thing you can do.

Travel and business were the two things in life that I desired most from my youngest days. I definitely did *not* want to get married and have kids; that seemed too hard. I never understood how you could look at someone and say, 'I would like to be with you in 20 years' time, in 50 years' time.' You don't even know if you will be living in the same country in 20 years' time!

My unassailable point of view was, 'I am not doing relationship — ever.'

Can you hear the question in that statement? No, because there isn't one; it is a total and utter conclusion. Every conclusion is a massive limitation. Whenever you have a conclusion about something, you cut infinite possibilities out of your life.

Let me give you an example. If someone has the conclusion that they are strictly vegetarian, they are creating a world of no-choice. I am not saying they have to go and eat meat. If you are a vegetarian by choice, then every day you would say, 'I prefer not to eat meat today. I prefer to be a vegetarian.'

It is a fresh choice that you make each day. You don't eat meat, but you have not eliminated it as a possibility from the menu of choices available to you.

Similarly, choosing to be in a relationship, or not, allows greater possibilities in your life.

By saying, 'I don't do relationship ever,' I had eliminated the choice to have a great relationship, a nurturing relationship and an empowering relationship.

Now I did not realise that I was functioning from no-choice until one day when I had a conversation with the founder of Access Consciousness®, Gary Douglas. I was talking to him about wanting to have sex with someone whom we both knew.

Gary's response was, 'He is mean and he will judge you.'

I replied, 'No, he is cute and he is awesome.'

Although it wasn't cognitive, this man would validate everything I had already decided was wrong about me. He was somebody who would judge me and my body the same way that I did. That was exactly the kind of person I chose to hook up with every single time, without thinking about why I chose this type of man.

Gary kept asking me questions about this man who I wanted to have sex with and the more questions he asked, the crankier and more petulant I got.

Finally, I put my hands on my hips and said, 'Great! So I just never get to have sex again?'

'Why would you say that?' Gary responded.

He went on to list three people who he said would be eager to have sex with me. I shrugged them off because they had never even crossed my mind.

Later on I discovered my point of view was that anyone who was eager to have sex with me must be a loser. The very fact they wanted to have sex with me, I had decided, was not appealing. Does that sound familiar?

If someone *didn't* want to have sex with me, and especially if they were judgemental, I considered them as winners. There was a third group of people, the 'no counts'. They were men who didn't lust after me or resist me. They just didn't count.

At some stage I had created these categories in my mind and automatically put the men I met into them. Strangely, this wasn't something I did cognitively. I didn't base it on how successful they were, their looks and characteristics or anything like that.

Then Gary said, 'Instead of wanting to have sex with this other person, you should sleep with Brendon.'

'What? Why?' I said.

Gary replied, 'Because then you will find out what it is like to be with someone who is kind, caring and nurturing.'

Now I had only met Brendon about six months before that. He fell into the category of 'no counts' because if you have ever met Brendon, you will realise there is no judgement in his world. He definitely did not judge my body. Strangely, this was one of the reasons why I was *not* attracted to him. I thought he was handsome and seemed nice, then again, I met so many different people all the time...

This conversation with Gary made me realise that in relationship I had been functioning from no-choice, even though I *thought* I was choosing to be with the men I desired. This was a huge awareness because

I finally got to see how much my point of view had been limiting me.

Since I desired to create my life from infinite possibilities, I knew I had to push down all my barriers to sex and relationship. I remember telling myself, 'Oh, I have to be like Switzerland. I have to be completely neutral. I have to have no point of view if I never have sex again, and no point of view if I have lots of sex; no point of view if I am in a relationship or not.'

As things played out, I ended up having sex with Brendon. It took a level of vulnerability for me to do this and from the first time, I was incredibly grateful. It didn't matter if we ever had sex again. I now knew the kind, caring and nurturing energy I desired to have in my life. Yet I also didn't have a desperate need to hold onto Brendon. If it led to something more — great.

The next morning, I told Gary, 'Wow. You are right. It was amazing *not* to be with someone who judges my body as much as I judge my body.'

Before, I had never, ever looked for someone who was kind and caring. Kind, caring and nurturing were just empty words to me; I had no idea what they actually were. To be honest, this was something I had not been willing to receive; I didn't think

I was worth it. It may sound like a cliché and yet I was actually living all of those clichés.

....

From the beginning, Brendon and I had a lot of fun together. All the same, I never found myself wondering, 'Is he going to call today? When are we going to see each other again?'

At the time I was travelling regularly to America, so I used two mobile phones. When I was in the United States, I hardly used my Australian phone. At most, I checked my messages about once a week. If there was a text from Brendon, I would reply. I wasn't intentionally playing hard to get! I love my work and creating my life. At one stage Brendon was thinking of flying to America to be with me as I had been away for quite some time. When he said that, I started to get butterflies in my stomach and heart palpitations because he is really sweet, really kind and so much fun to be around.

Brendon and I have lived together for about eight years and my life would not be as great as it is without him in it. The level of gratitude I have is for his very being. It is not for some monetary contribution; it is not the typical analysis of gratitude. That is what relationship should be based on — gratitude. Not on expectations and projections of each other.

If you look up the word relationship, you will find that is defined as the distance between two objects and ironically this is what most people in the world end up creating! When you first meet someone, you are yourself. Then all of a sudden, or perhaps one month later or six months later, you start cutting off parts of you in order to stay in the relationship. How often do people give up doing the things they love because it no longer fits their new status as a couple? This reality says, if you are in a relationship you should do everything together. I see so many people use their relationship to diminish themselves to the point where they can't rely on anything else but their relationship.

That is not what a relationship should be. Relationship should not be the distance between two objects. It should be a level of honouring of and gratitude for, and vulnerability and allowance with, the other person.

The reason for being with somebody else is so that you can create at least 20 times more than you would create alone. Being in a relationship can be an expansion of your very being, just by allowing the contribution that another person is to you and your life. Not many people talk about that.

Chapter 1 Tools

- What are your points of view on relationship? Do you avoid relationship since you can't see any good ones? Do you always pick partners who judge you and your body the same way you do?

'The level of gratitude I have is for Brendon's very being.'

Simone

CHAPTER 2

It's not your child's job to make you happy

Brendon

As a young boy it seemed to me that relationships were all about control and not about happiness. Either the man controlled the woman or the woman controlled the man. Someone always controlled the other person.

To the outside world I probably looked like a typical, carefree Aussie bloke who loved drinking beer and surfing. But all the while I was growing up my mum was in an abusive relationship with my dad. That was my first look at relationship.

Later, my mum got a new husband and I got to see a different kind of abuse. Although it wasn't as violent, there was verbal abuse — and monetary

SIMONE MILASAS & BRENDON WATT

abuse. There were so many fights and arguments over money that I began to hate money. By the time I was 18, relationship didn't interest me much.

Except that for most of my life I had felt like a round peg in a square hole. I was always looking at how I could fit into this reality and having a relationship seemed like a good way of fitting in.

Like most people, I learned about life from my parents. So what did I do when I decided to be in relationship? I chose a woman who was a lot like my father, very abusive. Somewhere in my world I decided that if I could figure out the abuse, then I could change it. It wasn't cognitive or something I thought through.

How was that relationship? Awful!

One of the things people do in a relationship is they tough it out. We are often told, 'You have got to stick it out. It is hard work; you have to work through things.'

No, you don't. If your relationship is not working, don't do it!

Although I know this now, back then I didn't know I had another choice. Even when this girl was not very nice to me, I decided to stay with her for 10 years. People usually have an agenda for getting

24

into relationships and my agenda was that if I could love my girlfriend enough she would finally stop acting so crazy and love me back. I was not very bright. But hey, I got my beautiful son, Nash, out of it.

The day I found out that Nash's mum was pregnant I remember thinking, 'This is fitting in. I have a girl-friend who I fight with all the time and don't get along with and now I am going to have a child.'

My bizarre logic was that by Nash coming into the world she would see that I loved her and our rela-tionship would start working. At the time I didn't realise what a huge unkindness it was to expect that my baby son would be the saviour of my life. Is it ever your child's job to make you happy?

As things turned out, when Nash was four years old I left his mother. For 10 years our relationship had been on and off. Every time we had a fight, I left her. Back then I wasn't willing to live on my own or see the value in me. Instead, I looked to other peo-ple for validation. So I kept going back to my girl-friend. She saw me as someone she could control and apparently back then I *liked* to be controlled.

One day I finally realised this on-off relationship had to end. When I left my girlfriend that final time, I knew that I would not be going back.

So at 30, I found myself living in my mother's house and sharing a bedroom with my four-year-old son. I was so miserable at one point I thought, 'How can I *not* live through this shit anymore?'

Then one day I saw an advertisement in the paper. It was a little pink advertisement that said, 'All of life comes to me with ease, joy and glory.' There was a girl's name and her phone number. I knew I had to call her.

When I went and saw this girl, she talked to me about something called the Access Bars®. She explained that it was a gentle technique that involved lightly touching my head. At that point I didn't care what she did, because I desperately needed help.

She got me to lay down on a massage table and ran my Bars. Afterwards, I went to my car but I didn't start it straight away. I sat there smiling for about 10 minutes. It was the first time I had felt truly happy or had really smiled in years. That day my life started to change.

I learned the Access Bars myself and I started going to more Access Consciousness classes. If you have ever been to an Access class then you will have noticed that there are lots of women and very few men. Back then my point of view was, 'If I got some more girls and more money then I will be happy!'

Anyone who knows me now, knows this is just not me. I knew a greater world was available. I just didn't know how to ask for it; I didn't know where to look for it. I didn't know what to do to get there. All I could think about was making my life slightly better by having more money and more girls.

Fast forward eight years and I am a little different. I recognise that what I desire is to create a better world — and I desire to be true to me no matter what that looks like.

The truth was that I had spent my life sitting around and waiting for God to come and scoop me up. He never did. After going to several Access classes, one day I realised that I had the tools to turn my life around, and I actually had to use them. It was time to get cracking and make different choices. That was another turning point in my life. I did not even dream back then that one day I would be facilitating Access Choice of Possibilities classes around the world.

......

In 2010 I met Simone at an Access class in Sydney. From the time we met, I was amazed by the way she looked at me and treated me. She saw in me the person that I was still unwilling to see. Talking about me to other people, she would say things like, 'Brendon is so brilliant. He is so great.' I used to think: 'who the hell is she looking at?' I judged myself hideously all the time for not having a lot of money, for living in my mum's house, for so many things that I had got wrong.

Simone was very different from any other woman I have met. For the first time in my life here was someone who did not want to control me. She is willing to let me do whatever I want to do. In the same way, I am willing to let her do whatever she wants to do, because I can see how great she is.

What we have is something different.

Simone and I have not said, 'We are in love now so everything is good.' That phrase: 'we are in love' is a conclusion. It is the pretence that you are going to be together forever. It is the assumption that the other person will never hurt you and you can always trust them. How often do you see that working?

Chapter 2 Tools

- Have you always known a greater world is available? Then use the tools in this book and start making different choices.

'One day I realised that I had the tools to turn my life around, and I actually had to use them.'

Brendon

CHAPTER 3

Today is what counts

Brendon

For a long time after getting together, Simone and I avoided calling what we had created 'a relationship'. From the outside people looked at us and assumed we were a couple. We kept saying, 'No we're not!' The subtext was, 'We are just friends who have sex and hang out.'

One day, I was at an Access Consciousness class in San Francisco, USA, where Gary talked about Simone and I being in relationship. I wanted to run out of the room.

The truth is that I was waiting for the hammer to fall.

I had experienced so much abuse in previous relationships that I knew eventually Simone was going to hurt me, which by the way is not a question.

But that is what people do in relationship. We have these trigger points based on our past. Any time there is a fight or an argument, you tell yourself, 'See, I was right. She is going to abuse me; she is going to leave me.'

A simple thing like Simone opening the bedroom door would make my heart drop. Not because of anything she would ever do, simply because that had been my experience. In the past someone walking into the room signalled fighting, anger, accusations and abuse. Unknowingly, I had held on to all these different situations in my life and had taken them into my new relationship with Simone.

So there we were, in relationship and avoiding relationship. Then one day Deb, my mum, came to my house. Simone and I were living together at the time, still avoiding relationship.

Mum said, 'I see the way you two are with each other. If I were looking for a relationship that is the sort of relationship I would want. You don't call it a relationship — so what the fuck is it?'

Her question stopped us in our tracks. We looked at each other and said, 'Maybe we should admit that we are in relationship.'

Simone

That was the moment when things changed a lot for me. Because in the early days, and unknown to each other, both of us were waiting for the abuse to start. I had been with men who continuously put me down and judged my body hideously and somewhere in my universe I was expecting Brendon to do the same. It was obvious to me. Brendon was going to ditch me, leave me or be mean to me. And I had better be ready for it. Although we never put it into words, that was actually why we both avoided relationship for the first couple of years we were together.

When we first met, I lived in a two-bedroom town house in Queensland, Australia. It really wasn't big enough for us especially as Brendon had his son, Nash, and a dog.

I used the second bedroom as an office and Nash would sometimes sleep there on the fold-out couch. One day I told Nash he needed to tidy up after himself and put his stuff away.

He asked me, 'Where do I put my stuff?'

I realised that he didn't have any place for his things so I went out and bought him a big plastic tub for his toys. This was taking one step closer to admitting that Brendon and I were in relationship and were willing to take on each other's commitments as well.

Eventually, Brendon started talking about getting a bigger house. This was it! Brendon had been living with me and now that he had got what he wanted, he was going to leave. I had expected that and so quite casually I asked him, 'Are you guys moving out?'

Brendon immediately said, 'With you, move out with you.'

Even though he said that, Brendon had some reservations about choosing to live together. To figure out what he truly desired as his future, he used one of the Access Consciousness tools.

For three whole days he imagined what his life would be like if we did *not* move in together.

Then, on the following three days, he indulged in the scenario of what his life would be like if he *did* move in with me. The second part didn't last three days. After only one day of indulging in the scenario of us living together he said, 'It is really obvious to me that my whole life would expand and we would create more if we were living together.'

I said, 'Okay, let's do it,' and left it at that. We didn't make it significant or plan the date when we would move in together. We just chose it. One day, shortly after we had come home from a seven-day Access Consciousness® class in New Zealand, I was un-packing my suitcase.

Brendon just looked at me and said, 'Honey, I need somewhere to put my clothes.'

I said, 'Are you moving in?'

He replied, 'Yep.'

That is how simple it was.

Brendon

A lot of us think we don't have the capacity for en-ergetic awareness. When you do something like in-dulging in two different scenarios for your future, you definitely realise that you have a capacity to perceive energy.

When I first used this tool, I immersed myself fully in the energy of not moving in with Simone. I would be planning to get my own place; I would have my son and my dog with me and so on. I did that for three consecutive days. There was no going back and forth.

After three days I switched foot and indulged in what it would be like to move in with Simone. Immediately I got the energy of the future that my choice would create. Within about five seconds I could sense my life expand and become greater and that is exactly what I had been asking for all along: a greater life.

The day Simone and I acknowledged we were in relationship, we had no idea what we were getting into, except that it matched the energy of the future we both desired to create. We had no clue what it would look like from day-to-day. We definitely weren't interested in creating relationship as we had in the past. So we made a commitment to ourselves to use the tools of Access to create something different.

As soon as we got to a place where the energy felt stuck, or heavy, we used one of the Access tools to change it. There were times when I thought, 'I so don't want to use that tool.' Since I knew the tools worked, I was willing to give them a go no matter how uncomfortable it was.

WHAT IF THERE WERE NO YESTERDAY IN RELATIONSHIP?

Relationship has to be a fresh choice every day.

It is about creation, contribution, being in allowance, having fun and being enthused about the adventure of your life. The moment you say that you *have* a relationship, you have quit creating it. You have defined it by saying, 'Oh, we live together; we're married; we're de facto.' etc. Every definition will create limitation in your life.

Definition does not exist within a question, so if you're willing to ask a question you have more choices available.

Simone and I live our lives based on questions: What can we choose today and what can we create together? We don't say we are going to be together for the next 20, or 30 years. There is no conclusion about where we are heading. We continuously play with different possibilities. We have a house, a child, a dog, a mortgage and so on; that still doesn't mean that we are locked into anything. Our relationship could end at any time — even though it would be an accounting nightmare!

I am not looking for Simone to make me happy. She knows that whatever I choose to get into, I will also choose to get out of. She has allowance for me and that allowance keeps me from trying to fix things for her, because a man's job is always to fix things.

We don't argue. I think we raised our voices to each other once. We have ease with each other because we have always found ease by using the tools in this book. We continue to use them all the time.

Gary Douglas says you are where you are today *not* because you have no money, or because of your relationship. You have created it by the choices you made. This was not easy for me to acknowledge at first. When I did, everything in my life changed quite dramatically. When I finally got that I had created all the unhappiness, the lack of work, by the choices I had made, I said, 'Whoa, what if I just started making some different choices?'

It was not comfortable to be brutally honest with myself and look at those big, bad, ugly secrets I had been hiding. Once I did, it allowed me to start moving forward in my life. I realised that I was in the driver's seat and I had to take control of the car.

If the same things keep repeating over and over in your life, look at what you love about them. Even if that means acknowledging that you are a complete asshole. Anything you hide from yourself will stop you. If you are willing to have the awareness of it, you can go beyond it.

Today is always a new day. What you did yesterday got you to where you were yesterday. What you choose today will be the things that will create your future.

If you want your future to be different and be greater, what choices do you need to make today? Start today, or don't. For me, sometimes I enjoy having a crappy day. Then I realise I am trying to go back into something that is familiar and comfortable. Lately, I am never, ever comfortable.

Chapter 3 Tools

- Does the same scenario keep occurring over and over in your relationships? If it does, look at what you love about it. Be honest with yourself, even if that means acknowledging you act like a complete asshole at times.

'Today is always a new day. What you did yesterday got you to where you were yesterday. What you choose today will be the things that will create your future.'

Brendon

CHAPTER 4

Creation of a future — in the now

Simone

For Brendon and me, relationship is not about growing old together or fulfilling each other's idea of the perfect partner.

The reason for being in a relationship with somebody is so that you create at least 20 times more in the world than you would create alone. Creation is endless. In creation, there is no definition; there is no limitation.

Brendon and I are building a house together, and like everything we are creating, it is not based on the necessity of having a roof above our heads.

Peregian Beach, where I live, has one of the most beautiful beaches in Queensland. Whenever I am at home I like to go jogging in the neighbourhood. There are about four blocks of land that I run past that I have always said I would buy, if they ever come up for sale. Well, one of them did. At the time we didn't have money sitting around to buy a block of land on the beach.

What I have noticed is that if either of us truly desires something, we don't stop the other person. Rather, we look at what we can contribute to make that happen for them.

When I told Brendon how I really wanted to buy this block of land on the beach, amazing man that he is, he started looking at what we would need to do and who we would need to talk to so that it became a reality.

We started with a build that matched the parameters of what we could 'afford'. Then we looked at what we would actually like to create on that beautiful block of land. I didn't want to build an 'affordable' house. It is like having a beautiful blank canvas and only using two colours to paint. No, I desire to paint with all the colours in my palette so I said to Brendon, 'Why can't we ask for what we really want?'

He replied, 'Good point.'

When we started meeting with architects and looking at what we would like to create, of course, the costs doubled. Yet we didn't slow ourselves down or stop in order to match what this reality projects at you if you ask for something that is considered too much. I want marble floors, a wine cellar, a gym… it will be an epic house and I am not having anything less.

It does take work though. We met with a few mortgage brokers and spoke to different people. Throughout this whole process we keep asking ourselves: 'What do we need to be to have this physically actualise and be our reality of what we would like to create?'

Instead of buying into any so-called 'problems' we are willing to change whatever we must change to create greater possibilities. I see so many people give up and stop when they see a problem rather than take two, three, five more steps to create what they actually desire.

THE EXUBERANCE OF CREATING TOGETHER

Brendon and I will talk about all the things we are creating together, yet it is not done from the expectation of being together forever. That may seem counter-intuitive and it is also one of the greatest gifts in our relationship. We wake up every morning and ask: 'What can we create together?'

Often, people will look at our relationship and say, 'I wish I could create more with my partner like Brendon and you do.'

I invariably ask them, 'What have you defined as creation?'

Creation is not about always doing everything together.

Whenever I am at home, I am really happy to go to the local farmers' markets at 5am and buy beautiful fresh produce. Most of the time Brendon is the one who cooks it. Although every now and then he will come to the markets with me, I never expect him to do so. He loves to sleep in.

People often misidentify that creating together means we both must get up and go to the markets together; we both must cook a meal together. That is not creation as contribution and contribution as creation. Creation is the willingness to contribute your capacities to create something greater and create more ease in your lives.

If Brendon travels overseas and I stay at home, we are still creating together. Creation is this continuous contribution to each other. If you are not always in the creative energy of a relationship, you will get bored.

One of the Access tools that I use every single day is to destroy and uncreate my relationship with Brendon. When you ask to destroy and uncreate your relationship, what you are doing is destroying every point of view you created about that person. Every limitation, every conclusion, every feeling you have about that person and your relationship, what you think it should be and what you have decided it should be: destroy and uncreate it all. There is a level of vulnerability with this; you are totally un-tethered from the past. What I aim for is to wake up every morning with the sense of, how did I get so lucky to have Brendon in my life?

Brendon

A relationship just doesn't happen. You get to cre-ate it fresh every day.

Every day, Simone and I both look at, 'What now? What is next? Who the hell am I today and what am I going to create?'

We don't look at who we were yesterday or what we did in the past. It is the total exuberance of, 'I am alive today. What do I wish to create with this person? What do I wish to create in this relationship?' and even, 'Do we still wish to be together today?'

When two people get together, usually they, their friends and family all expect them to stay together and live out their lives in a certain pattern. There is a certain order to relationships in this reality. We know it well because people often project at us the view that: 'Well, now you have your house, you have your dog, you have got your child…This is it. This is the finale. It is time to get the matching rocking chairs.'

In the past eight years, not once have Simone and I looked at our relationship as a long-term thing or thought that we will grow old together. Both of us knew that having such an expectation would drive the other one away.

We desire to create a relationship that goes beyond any definitions and limitations. We function from the fluidity of constantly asking: 'Is this what we desire today?' and if the answer is 'yes,' the next question is: 'What can we create together?'

This is very different to how most people learn to function in relationship. I see a lot of people using projections and expectations with their partners. It might be that the man needs to earn x amount of money or the woman needs to cook dinner four nights a week. I was talking to a lady recently who said she had asked her husband to make dinner and when he didn't, she became very angry with him.

I said, 'Okay, tell me how you asked him.'

She said, 'I emailed him and I said, "I am running late so you need to make dinner."'

That is *not* asking someone for help. How is sending an email to your partner saying, 'I am running late and I need you to make dinner,' delivered with so much energy, a question? It isn't.

These are some of the ways that we try and control our relationships. What if you started looking at being a contribution to each other instead?

Chapter 4 Tools

- Every single day destroy and uncreate your relationship with your partner. What occurs is that you will destroy every point of view, every limitation, every conclusion and every feeling you have about them and your relationship. That is how you become untethered from the past and create your relationship as a fresh choice every day.

'Creation is this continuous contribution to each other. If you are not always in the creative energy of a relationship, you will get bored.'

Simone

CHAPTER 5

Creating a connection

Simone

Quite some years ago, I was chatting with a rather attractive guy I had met, and in the course of the conversation, we discovered that both of us had lived in the same area in Sydney and had been to many of the same parties. There was this moment where we both looked at each other like: *'Ahh! I know you!'*

In that same instant, I realised just because I had a fairly good sense of some of the things he had done, it didn't mean we were now best friends. Those were the points where our lives and choices had intersected. Overall, those points of connection didn't hold any great significance.

When people say, 'I am searching for The One,' or 'I have found The One,' they are talking about points of connection, which actually are a limitation. When you look for connection, you give up creation for familiarity, for what you know. It is like having a checklist: *Does he or she smoke cigarettes? Oh look, I smoke cigarettes too. I snore, he snores. I hate housework, they hate housework.* If you find yourself looking for points of connection in a relationship — run!

Brendon and I are more interested in what we can create together, so we are always looking for points of creation, not the points of connection, because in truth, you are *not* going to have a perfect relationship. You are not going to find the perfect partner because they do not exist. Perfection is a judgement.

When I was in my twenties, I had an affair with a 55-year-old mountaineer who I met in Nepal. My friends said, 'Oh, he is so old. He is 55.' His age didn't matter to me. He was lots of fun to be with and he inspired me to be something different.

Later, when I was in my thirties, I went out with an 18-year-old man. Again, my friends were quite shocked. They said, 'Oh my god. He just got out of school!'

What if the person you choose to be in relationship with is not based on age, gender, looks, colour, creed or financial reality? What if it was about the fun factor and the joy of creation and the five elements of intimacy? These five elements are honour, gratitude, allowance, trust and vulnerability and we will introduce them to you later on in this book.

NOT EVERYONE CREATES IN THE SAME WAY

Brendon

Simone said something to me that changed my whole life — and at the time I wanted to kill her.

One day I was in the shower when she said, 'You know what? You don't really create; you do other things. You don't really create.'

I stood in the shower, fuming and swearing, 'Fuck you!'

Now just before this conversation, I had been thinking about going on the reality TV cooking show *MasterChef Australia*. So as soon as I got out of the shower, I filled out the whole application, made videos, sent it in and eventually got selected to be one of the top 100 contestants for *MasterChef Australia*.

When Simone said I didn't create, she pissed me off so much that I thought, 'I will show her I can create.' She didn't say it from unkindness; that was simply her point of view at the time.

What she said to me that day changed my life and motivated me beyond what anything else has ever done in the past. In that moment, not only did I resist and react to what she said, I also made a different demand in my world. Creation is a demand you have to make of yourself. From that day forward, I have created so much more in my life.

Simone

There are certain people who are an energetic contribution, just by being the kindness, caring and brilliance that they are. When I told Brendon that he didn't create, I meant he was one of those people who contribute energetically, which is the energy of creation.

I am also grateful that things occurred like that because this energy was required to get Brendon to create. Through his creations, Brendon has been a massive inspiration to me to create even greater. It is a bit like playing a game that in Australia we call leapfrog, where one person jumps forward and the next person jumps over the top of them. Each one takes turns to go further and further. That is truly what relationship and creation should be. You continually inspire and enthuse the other person to be greater every day; to claim, own and acknowledge all the capacities they have that they are not willing to acknowledge, while not judging them if they don't choose to do so.

Brendon

Creating in relationship is the willingness to contribute your energy to whatever the other person desires to create. If you both desire to create the same thing and go down the same track, then you both contribute energy to each other.

Some people think that working on the same project together means they get to control the other person. That is not creating; that is control. If you desire a relationship where you can create together then ask your partner, 'How can I contribute to you?' If you are willing to contribute energy, you can actually have a relationship that is creative.

Simone and I create on our own and we always include the other one in it. Creating together would drive me mad. Simone is not allowed in the kitchen because the way she cooks frustrates me — kidding!

We definitely have a similar target: always create more. We are willing to look far enough into the future to see what else is required for the life we desire to create together.

There was a time when I used to make myself wrong for not creating like Simone does. She is incredibly creative. When she gets new information, she knows this piece needs to go here and that piece needs to go there. For her it is like moving chess pieces around the board.

When I get information, I let it sit in my awareness and usually I will distract myself with something else while allowing things to fall into place. I might play a game, or watch TV, as a way of creating some space for my ideas to fall into place.

Over the years I have heard so many people say, 'I was in the shower and I came up with this great idea...'

I used to wonder what they do in the shower. Because, I go into the shower and wash myself. I don't think about anything. Everyone was saying, 'Yeah, I came up with this awesome idea in the shower today,' and I kept thinking, 'Fuck, am I doing showering wrong?'

Simone

That is funny and yet so true! Just because someone is your partner, or your Enjoyable Other as I like to say, that doesn't mean they have to create like you do. No two people will create in the same way. Your partner doesn't have to create at the same speed, or with the same thoughts.

I am really creative in the morning, almost from the moment I wake up, and less so in the evenings. For me creation is extrapolation. I love to throw ideas around. We may use some of them. We may not. The overriding theme is, 'What are we going to create? What can we choose that is going to work or create a different possibility?' And it is fast. That is how I like to create.

A couple of years ago, Brendon and I were in Cancun, Mexico, when we had an 'almost-argument.' At the time we were thinking about buying a second house and Brendon simply put his foot down and said, 'No. We are not doing it.' There was no extrapolation of ideas or talking about the possibilities that buying this house could create in our lives.

What I later realised was that a man does not sit around extrapolating all the time. Men will do it on their own. They will do it in silence. They will create something and then say, 'This is what it is going to be.'

So from this almost-argument I got a new tool and that is to ask Brendon to include me in the creation. That is where you literally ask someone, 'Hey, can you tell me how you got to that result?'

Brendon

When Simone and I were talking about finances in Cancun, we got to a place that was not generative. We both felt the energy contract and recognised that we needed to stop talking about it right away.

We had started butting heads and our different points of view on finances were contracting our energy, rather than expanding it. When Simone and I became aware that the conversation was not going anywhere, we immediately started asking questions: 'Do we require more information, yes or no? Yes? From whom could we get that information?'

We both knew that we could talk to Gary Douglas, or some of our other friends who are brilliant with finances and get these extra bits of information from them. Since nothing was going to change right away, we went and had a glass or two of wine as we didn't want to make a problem of something that wasn't a problem. We both knew that when we had more information, we could create something greater. So rather than argue, we chose to enjoy each other and have fun.

A lot of research has been done about couples fighting over money and finances and the stress it causes in a relationship. They have even done studies to show that money stress is a major factor in divorce.

When you are willing to be aware of any contraction in your relationship, you won't go into who is right and who is wrong. You won't start a fight. Instead, you will look at what will create a sense of expansion again. The pragmatics of relationship is looking at: 'What is going to work here? What can I do to create more in this relationship?'

Simone and I have many examples of times where things weren't really working and we changed the energy, rather than go to fight.

We are taught, or else we buy the lie, that fighting is normal in relationship. In eight years, Simone and I have not had one fight. Some people think we are crazy or there is something wrong with us because we don't argue our points of view. We are more interested in looking at, how can we change the energy of this situation?

Chapter 5 Tools

- If you desire a relationship where you can create together, then ask your partner: 'How can I contribute to you?'

- Acknowledge that people create in different ways.

- Always inspire and enthuse your partner to be greater every day; to claim, own and acknowledge all the capacities they have, yet don't judge them if they don't choose to do so.

'Creation is a demand you have to make of yourself.'

Brendon

CHAPTER 6

Who is paying?

Simone

When I first met Brendon, I earned a lot more money than he did. At the time he was a tiler, or a 'tradie' as they are called in Australia.

Brendon hated his job and I couldn't watch someone who is such a contribution to me, do what he hates just to bring home some money. So I suggested to Brendon that he look for something else to do while I supported him.

I didn't put a time limit on it. Rather, every day I looked at our relationship and asked many questions: 'Is this relationship a contribution to my life? Is it a contribution to my living? Is it a contribution to my body?' The awareness I received was yes, yes, yes.

Brendon came with the whole package. His son, Nash, was then five years old and there was Max, the dog. For someone who never desired to have a relationship, I suddenly had the lot.

Agreeing to support Brendon was not much of a challenge because I liked being the one who earned more money. It gave me a sense of control and the choice to leave at any second. I knew it would be easy to orchestrate things so they turned out the way I wanted them to, if I ever wanted to leave. Looking back, I can see this was a level of cruelty and unkindness to him and me. Back then I was still waiting for the shoe to drop; I was waiting for the day when we would say, 'This is all over.'

So, I used money as a way of separation by keeping tabs on what we were spending. If the dog food cost $20, my point of view was that Brendon should pay for it. This might seem familiar to some people. You may recognise where you are doing something similar in your relationship.

We had a Google document with all of the things I was buying with my money — it was *my* money at that stage. I put it all down: flights to Costa Rica, accommodation, even the dog food! As the months went past, the amount I was owed gradually increased. It got to about $20,000, so one day I looked at Brendon and said, 'Are you ever going to pay this or do I just delete this Google document?'

'Just delete it,' he replied.

From that moment we started being more in communion with each other because previously both of us had used money as a way to create separation: me earning more; he earning less.

I am not saying that if you are in a relationship you must have joint bank accounts, or do everything that we have done. You have to choose what works for you. Don't base it on the need for control or separation, because separation is a total rejection of you and them.

BEING VULNERABLE AND ASKING FOR HELP

Simone

During this time while I was paying for everything, Brendon was waking up in the mornings depressed. He was picking up on all the sadness and depression in the world and thinking *he* was sad and depressed. He would lie on the couch and drink beer while I was working. It got to the point where I was running out of money.

Brendon

I was spending it all.

Simone

Yes, you were!

One of the tools that Gary gave me to use when I got cranky at Brendon for spending all the money, was to ask for his help. So one day I sat down with Brendon and showed him all the bills.

I showed him everything and said, 'This is the rent that we are paying (which meant this is the money I am paying). This is the money we are spending (which meant this is the money you are spending).'

It wasn't the easiest thing for me to do. I knew that if I were asking him for help, I had to be vulnerable with myself and with him. So I also showed him all my bank accounts and all of the finances so he could have an awareness of what was being created and could contribute to that as well, and it wouldn't just be on my shoulders.

In many relationships there is this unspoken notion that we have to hide our finances. We are more willing to talk about the money we spend, yet society projects at us that we should hide the amount of money we make. I did not want to hide anything from Brendon. I knew that to change the financial reality we had together and create something greater, I had to be willing to show him everything and that is what I did.

At the same time, I didn't have any points of view or expectations of Brendon. He could do anything with the information. I knew he was smart and really good with numbers. He was not using those capacities back then and yet they were there, dormant. From the beginning I saw how great Brendon was, even though he refused to see it himself, and I was willing for him to choose it or not. That always had to be his choice and will always be his choice.

....

The dynamic of money and relationships is very interesting. Many people refuse to look at this even though it can be quite revealing. I have come across women who are waiting for a man to come along and supply them with the money they have decided they need but cannot create on their own. I have also met men who were trained to believe that their job is to find a woman, then go to work and create the money for their relationship.

How many lifetimes have you been a man? How many lifetimes have you been a woman? If you realise that you have been both a man and a woman in different lifetimes, then you will see how your choices get limited by different points of view.

Have you heard people say, 'The man is the breadwinner,' or 'Women can't earn more than men'?

Those points of view will keep you stuck and prevent you from moving forward.

What I would love you to get out of this book is the choice of possibilities that are available to you. You don't have to be limited to the expectations, the projections and the judgements that define relationship in this world. Know you have the choice to create a relationship that is way beyond where you are currently functioning from.

Brendon and I continually give ourselves the choice to choose, the choice to change, the choice to not be together. In fact, the first time we bought a house together, I panicked because I thought it meant we had to be together forever.

'It is just a house,' Brendon pointed out. 'We can always sell it.'

Once I looked at it as a business deal, I was fine with it.

Even though our relationship is a fresh choice that we make every day, we have bought real estate together; we have a successful stock portfolio. As we write this book, we have purchased two luxury homes and are in the midst of building a third, which is pushing the limits of what we *thought* we could create. We know that this is just the tip of the iceberg. None of these things would have occurred if I had held on to my point of view that I couldn't buy a house with this man because that meant being together forever.

Everyone has insane points of view that lock them up and don't allow them to create a greater life. It is those insane points of view that you must become aware of and change, because they are the invisible agendas and problems that run your life. How many of you are using the problem you have decided you cannot overcome to *not* push the boundaries of your limitations and create something greater?

How many insane points of view, agendas and problems do you have that keep you from creating relationships and money?

Some people have an agenda about finding a partner to supply them with everything they have decided they need. How many needy agendas do you have of your partner, be they a man or a woman? It could be you need them to supply you with money so you can stay at home and look after the kids, or it could be the other way around.

Do you have the agenda of creating no money in order to control your life? If you don't have all the money you desire and require, you are creating that by your points of view. That means you are the one who has to change your points of view. No one else can do it for you.

Chapter 6 Tools

- What is the problem you have decided you cannot overcome? Have you been using that as an excuse for not pushing the boundaries of your limitations and creating something greater?

'If you don't have all the money you desire and require, you are creating that by your points of view.'

Simone

CHAPTER 7

I used to hate money

Brendon

What is your relationship with money? Do you love it or hate it? Do you want to run away from money?

In the past I did not have a very good relationship with money. In fact, I hated it. As a boy, I watched the people around me constantly argue and fight over money. I saw so much monetary abuse that before I was 10 years old, I subconsciously decided that I would avoid it at all costs. That one decision had a massive impact on my life.

When I was about 17 years old, I moved out of home and started a job. Each Friday when I got paid I would spend so rapidly that by Monday all my money was gone. Any time I got a bill in the mail, I chucked it straight into the bin without opening it.

If my phone rang and there was no caller ID, I hung up, because that usually meant debt collectors.

At one point my electricity was cut off as I hadn't paid the bill — I probably hadn't even opened it. At the time I was living in a unit and my flatmate was out of town, so I couldn't get a loan to pay it either. What did I do? I got an extension power cord and plugged it into the outlet in the hallway so I could run my fridge — sweet! That was just one of the many creative ways I avoided money. Yet cognitively, I didn't realise the full impact of my actions.

As the debts piled up, the thought of paying off such a large debt seemed so impossible, I buried my head in the sand and refused to even think about it.

Then, not long after Simone and I had bought a house together, I casually mentioned that I had a rather large tax bill. She asked me how much it was.

'Over $200,000,' I replied.

'Isn't that something you would tell someone *before* you move in with them?' she asked.

When Simone made that comment, I saw that she actually had a point. I had acted like a total asshole by waiting till *after* we bought a house together to tell her about my debt.

That was the moment I realised I had been avoiding money dynamically because when I was younger, every time money was mentioned it ended in yelling, screaming and fighting. At a young age I decided that money equalled abuse. What I didn't acknowledge was that choosing to have no money is also abuse, just a different kind of abuse.

Becoming aware that I had been avoiding money was a huge revelation to me. Before that, I didn't know how to change what was going on with my finances. It had felt literally impossible. When I started getting clear on what I had created, the energy of 'impossible' went away. If I had created this massive debt by the choices I had made, then what if I started making some different choices?

The first person I turned to was Simone.

'Can you help me?' I asked her, 'I don't know what to do here.'

She suggested that we meet with an accountant and try and get a payment plan to pay off the debt. When that was refused, I was forced to declare bankruptcy. First, I looked at every single scenario where this choice could and couldn't affect my life. I read a lot of information, talked to accountants and people knowledgeable in this area. It is a big choice and I highly recommend that you don't overlook anything when doing your homework.

FINANCIAL 101 CATCH-UPS

Simone

Brendon's willingness to have clarity on his financial situation created huge amounts of change for him. It created massive change for me also. I realised that I was deeply committed to him and what we are creating together.

I could have told Brendon, 'You are on your own with your debt.' That did not match the energy of what I wished to create. Our relationship is not based on telling the other person what they should do or be, it is based on allowance and empowering each other to be greater.

So, I used to drag Brendon along to meetings with our accountants. He hated it and wanted to run out of the door as soon as we had finished.

Later, we started having informal sessions with our friends Steve and Chutisa Bowman. We would often go to a great restaurant, have some great champagne and ask them questions about money and business. We called it our 'Financial 101' catch-ups.

If someone you know is creating a lot, I highly recommend you have a chat with them. Buy them dinner or drinks and ask lots of questions about what they are choosing so that you can increase your financial awareness.

Both the Bowmans had worked in the corporate world for many years. They have chosen to create a business so that they can create more wealth together. In fact, they have started many businesses that have been extremely successful. Now, they travel the world and do seminars together.

At first when we met with the Bowmans for these Financial 101 sessions, Brendon wanted to fall asleep or drink too much. He did everything he could to avoid the topic of money.

I knew the energy of avoidance well because once upon a time that was how I had functioned. Years prior, my father tried to teach me about money, finances and book keeping. He was an accountant. Whenever he tried to talk to me about the financial side of business, I used to get cranky and petulant and say I didn't want to know about those boring things; I just wanted to create. He would point to the profit and loss statement and say, 'You can't have your creations unless you know about this too.'

Since I had been there and done that, I recognised the energy Brendon was exuding. As with any of the Access tools, when you are willing to be aware of a limitation or fixed point of view, you can change it. When you are not willing to be aware of it, you cannot. You do detriment to yourself when you avoid things. Rather than acknowledging to yourself, 'Okay, I am going to be totally honest with myself and have the courage to look at what I have currently created, and then look at what I can change,' be that in the area of money, business, relationship, sex, your body or any area in life.

Avoiding the topic of money is avoiding the topic of creation. Money is the tool that allows you to create more in life. It is not the source of creation — you are the source of creation. If you are refusing to look at money, if you are refusing to receive money, if you are refusing to talk about money, then you are refusing to be the source of creation.

So many people say they want to have freedom, clarity and more ease with money. Yet every time they refuse to look at something, or talk about it, they are avoiding the freedom they could have in that area.

For me, any time I get funky around money or use money to create a strangeness in our relationship, I know there is something I must look at. This occurred during an Access Consciousness 7-day class that Brendon and I were attending in India. As soon as I became aware of that energy, I said to him, 'Can we have a chat? I am getting funky about money.'

Brendon looked at me and said, 'I thought we already had this discussion? Your money is *our* money. I thought we already knew that.'

I started laughing because of the dry way he said it. Also, the energies behind his words were the energies of gifting, contribution and creation rather than the energy of 'take' and I clearly perceived that.

In that moment I became aware of the sense of communion Brendon and I have and create continually. It is not based on money. It is based on creating a future that works for both of us that isn't about money, although it allows money to show up.

I saw all the different places and ways in which Brendon was contributing that weren't necessarily monetarily, yet they were a massive contribution nevertheless. I recalled the times where I had been working on my computer all day and late at night, sitting at the kitchen bench with a glass of wine, while he cooked us a fabulous meal. That, to me, is creating together. That, to me, is the contribution we both can be while enjoying what we each do.

Brendon will cook a meal and spend hours making a beautiful sauce. If I tried to do that I would find it one of the most frustrating things in the world. Sitting at the kitchen bench and watching him cook is fun, while I work on my computer and create what I enjoy.

What if you could choose what is fun for you, what brings you joy, and then contribute to each other from that space? That will create something far greater in your life than choosing not to be in a relationship.

Another example of this is the first time we did renovations on our home. Brendon oversaw the whole thing. He even did some of the tiling and created one of the most amazing bathrooms I have ever seen. Now, with this block of land on the beach that we bought (with private beach access!), that is an incredible creation on both our parts because we both demanded more in our lives.

This time Brendon won't be on the tools or doing the tiling because he doesn't need to be. It is not a necessity. Now, he would choose to hire a project manager to run it while he travels the world, empowering people. That is a choice and a preference he would make.

Being able to do something out of choice rather than necessity is a whole new realm of possibility. Previously, he wasn't very busy. He would cook these beautiful meals at night and oversee the renovations of our house. My life wouldn't be as big as it is today if he hadn't contributed things like that. You can do this in your own relationship too. Look at who is contributing monetarily and who is contributing things that are an expansion of your relationship together.

The other side of that is, once Brendon started earning more money and travelling the world without me, I began to question if he still needed me. I almost created a sense of break-up in our relationship until I realised that Brendon is with me simply because he chooses to be with me. Not because he needs my money. Rather, he loves hanging out with me and he loves creating with me. It has called for me to become even more vulnerable. It is a totally new level of caring that I have had to step into — and I am welcoming every moment of it.

Chapter 7 Tools

- What is your relationship with money?
- Do you love it or hate it?
- Do you avoid money?

'Avoiding the topic of money is avoiding the topic of creation.'

Simone

CHAPTER 8

Can I have the money now?

Brendon

The turning point for me was the day I finally realised that the people around me who had money were having way more fun than my broke ass!

For 30 years I had done ignorance with money and stupidity with money. To be honest, I had had enough. So I started looking at changing my points of view. Would it be fun to have money? What would it be like if I stopped avoiding it, stopped hating it and started creating it?

Getting rid of my old points of view was just the first step. The second one was education. Like so many people I had not been educated about money. I had no idea how to make it, or how to manage it. I saw money as the cash that came out of the hole in the wall, the ATM. Money is not only cash.

It can be a million different things. Money can be someone buying you lunch, because you are still receiving some sort of revenue.

I would love to say that educating myself about money was this fun, wonderful thing. At the start, I hated it! I had so many doubts about myself and what I was capable of. I didn't think I was smart enough or educated enough, since I was 'just a tradie'. All these doubts were the things I had decided were true in order to keep myself poor. If I changed my point of view, would I also change my life?

The good news is life can spin around quickly if you are willing to make a different choice and make a demand of yourself. Also, be kind to yourself when you go back to your old ways, as I periodically did.

Simone was patient with me. She knew that I was willing to have money; I just hadn't learned that I could choose my life. I hadn't yet learned that happiness was a choice. We would go and meet with our accountants and within five minutes I wanted to run away. My point of view was, 'Get me out of here. This is so boring.'

Since I had made the demand to change my money situation, I was persistent. Whenever the energy of wanting to avoid money came up, I acknowledged it. For instance, if opening my credit card statement made me seriously angry, frustrated, or uncomfortable, I would sit with those energies and see what, if anything, I could change.

Changing something that I had pushed away for so long didn't happen in an instant. Yet I was not going to run away from it or avoid it anymore. I sat with that energy of discomfort, as frustrating as that was.

Eventually, I got to the place where I became curious about money. I started to explore how finances and investments worked. That is really how I turned around my money situation. The biggest thing was realising what was limiting me, and then being honest with myself. This allowed me to see that while Simone had been avoiding relationship, I had been avoiding relationship *and* money. I had the double whammy.

If you want a greater life, you must be brutally honest even if you have to admit, 'Okay, I am a complete asshole'. You don't have to tell anyone or give up all your big, bad, ugly secrets. Since those big, bad, ugly secrets may be stopping you from moving forward in your life, do not lie to yourself. As soon as you lie to yourself, you cut off your awareness and get stuck in your own story. If you hide something or are unwilling to look at it, you cannot go beyond it.

So many people say, 'I have this money problem, why can't this change?' Let me ask you, is it actually yours? It was quite liberating to realise that 99 percent of all the points of view I had about money were not even mine; they belonged to other people. The people I grew up around. The kids I went to school with and the friends I hung out with.

If you look back over your life as a child and see the way people around you functioned with money, you will easily spot the times when you made certain decisions that had an impact on your future. The good news is, once you recognise those are simply points of view, you can change them.

If you would like more money in your life then you have to make different choices. A lot of people think choice means saying the words, 'I am choosing to have more money' Then they stay at home watching *Game of Thrones* on TV all day long.

That is not making a choice! If you desire to make $1,000, be willing to go out and do whatever it takes to create that money. Find a second job, become an Uber driver, or do whatever is fun for you that will bring in money.

Another thing to remember is that if you set a target and get there, please acknowledge what you have created. Your life will start moving and once it is moving in that forward way, it will get faster, yet you must start with these things.

NOBODY NEEDS TO HAVE A MONEY PROBLEM

Simone

At one point I asked Brendon, 'What if you were the Chief Financial Officer (CFO) of our companies?' We have a bunch of companies in trust which we use for various investments to create our financial reality. In the business world, the CFO is the one who constantly looks at what will expand, grow and make more money for the business with ease. I can do that, even though it isn't something I totally enjoy. What is more fun for me, is creating money.

So, Brendon took over that and now he handles everything to do with our money, our investments and so on. In the past I used to control all of the money that I created.

There are many tools and suggestions in this book, not all of them are easy. Most of them were not the easiest choice to make at the time. Yet every single choice has allowed something to show up that was greater than before.

Allowing Brendon to take control and handle all of our finances was not an easy choice for me. I had to learn to choose a different energy, since I was so used to having total control. What helped was the realisation that if I let go of total control, I would not only have my awareness, I would also have *his* awareness of what we could create.

And, what we have created together is phenomenal. I doubt that I would have created as quickly without having Brendon in my life and part of the finances of Milasas Watt. In truth nobody needs to have a money problem. You can create a greater outcome, and a greater income, if you are actually willing to work on the topic of money together.

Brendon and I have a fun little tool that we use if either one of us gets funky about money — the other one goes shopping! It is a little game we play to remind ourselves that there are a whole lot of money tools available; you don't have to have a money problem. If I get funky with money, Brendon will go online and go shopping. Or, I will do the same thing. It is amazing how quickly we get over our supposed money problem!

Getting to the stage where I was willing for Brendon to lose everything, so that we could actually have everything, was not an easy choice. And, I can say that if you allow yourself to make choices like this, what gets created is a very different reality. It is fun and that is what relationship should be. Also, be willing to change the energy when it gets stuck and funky. I have a friend who has a very creative way of handling this. When she and her partner get funky about money, they get naked in whatever room they are at the time, be it the lounge room, the kitchen or the bedroom. They take their clothes off and start talking about money, which usually makes them laugh. My suggestion is for you to find the tool that works for you, something that will take the *problem* out of the money issue you are having and actually turn it into a possibility and the gift of possibility you can choose with someone else.

Chapter 8 Tools

- If you would like more money start making different choices: Find a second job; become an Uber driver; or do whatever will be fun *and* bring in money.

'Be kind to yourself if you go back to your old ways, as I periodically did.'

Brendon

CHAPTER 9

Sex for the fun of it

Simone

Money and sex are probably the least talked about aspects of relationship. The most secret, the most hidden, the most complicated — and it doesn't have to be complicated.

Attitudes to sex get formed quite early on. Have you ever noticed how girls are taught to look for a relationship from a young age and are strongly discouraged from having random sex?

When it comes to sex there is something called the 1-2-3 rule. Imagine you see someone across a crowded room and end up having random sex for the fun of it. Because sex is considered so significant in our society, you start to think about what it all means and what it should look like and when you will see them again. Even if you don't do it cognitively, you start to create the story of what it would be like if you were married to this person.

The first time you have sex with someone is always for fun. By the second time, you are already in relationship with them. By the third time, you are subconsciously considering marriage. You have already started to create the story of what life would be like if you were married to them. That is what occurs for a majority of people. I am not saying it has to be true for you. What if every single time you had sex, it didn't mean anything or have to lead to something?

Choosing sex for the sheer fun of it can be just a choice, the same as choosing to be in relationship or not. Yet many women have it all worked out. They have all these ideals about the perfect relationship for them: the job their man will do, the car they will drive, the university they will have attended. Some have even picked out the white wedding gown they would like to wear one day.

What is on your wish list for your ideal mate? Have you decided it has to be a man or a woman? Do they have to live in the same country? Have you decided they have to be older than you or richer than you? How many women, secretly, do not desire to have a partner who is shorter than they are? Every decision is a limitation.

Had I been asking for Brendon to show up, my wish list would have included things like, 'Someone who is 11 years younger than me, has a child, is $200,000 in debt, snores, smokes...'

Brendon

I was the perfect catch!

It is so true. If Simone had written a wish list of *her* ideal man she might have written things like: 'He can't smoke, he can't have a kid, he can't have debt, he can't...' and then she wouldn't have been able to receive me.

If you must have a list of attributes or characteristics you desire in a future partner, here are three things that Gary Douglas came up with:

1. Someone who contributes monetarily (this could be similar to me contributing to Simone's life and living so she would have more time to create money),

2. Someone who lets you do whatever the hell you want and you let them do whatever the hell they want,

3. They are good in bed.

When it comes to sex, people love to do this thing that in Access we call crotch-tripping. That is where they make pretty much everything about sex. The meaning of the whole relationship is based on sex, whether you are having sex or not having sex; how often you are doing it every week, etc.

Then there is another category called head-tripping. That is when, after you have sex with someone, you constantly think about when they are going to call you or what they are going to do next. You have all this mind chatter going on based on the point of view that because you had sex with someone, other things will happen. In your head you are always thinking, 'Are they going to call me? Are they going to do this?'

Simone

There is a third one called heart-tripping. For instance, if your lover didn't give you flowers on Valentine's Day, what does that mean? Or if he *did* give you flowers on Valentine's Day, what does it mean? Did he give you 12 dozen roses or a single red rose? Or if you were at a party and your girlfriend didn't kiss you when she got there, what does it mean? Everything *means* something. I know this one well, because out of all three, I was the heart-tripper.

The interesting thing is people think that heart-tripping, head-tripping or crotch-tripping will help them with their relationships. So, if you are a head-tripper, you think that working out your relationship will give you clarity. In fact it doesn't give you clarity at all, although it will keep you going round and round in circles, constantly thinking about the meaning of every single thing that occurs.

Making everything meaningful will limit what can show up for you. Take the convention of a man giving flowers to a woman on anniversaries and birthdays. If I expected Brendon to give me flowers, I would be very disappointed all the time. Brendon doesn't do that.

And, there have been times when he gave me flowers spontaneously and they were incredible. I remember a time when we were in Rome, Italy, staying in a huge apartment. One day Brendon was leaning over the balcony, having a cigarette. In Rome there are these guys who walk around all the time, selling flowers. So, Brendon leaned over the balcony and yelled out to the guy to wait. Then he ran downstairs and got two dozen long-stemmed red roses at a ridiculous price, and casually came back upstairs. The next thing I knew the concierge was at the door and he had these beautiful flowers for me in a vase. It was so unexpected and so much fun!

Another time, Brendon gave me flowers after I had a major operation. I had been getting frustrated that it was taking so long for me to heal and start working again. I thought I was a burden to everyone around me. So many crazy points of view came up. The next day when Brendon came home he brought me a massive bunch of flowers. He walked up to the veranda where I was and gave me the flowers and a beautiful card; I burst out crying. He wrote in the card that I would never be a burden in his life and that I was always such an inspiration to him.

When you are in allowance of your partner, no matter what they choose, then you can receive their random acts of kindness. If I had the point of view that Brendon had to give me flowers on my birthday or on Valentine's Day, and I got upset when he didn't, I would not be able to receive the times when he spontaneously chooses to gift me flowers.

....

With head-tripping, heart-tripping and crotch-tripping, if you have been doing that your whole adult life and would like to change, first you must get over the point of view that it actually will create anything other than confusion. Otherwise you will keep doing it over and over in different relationships. Look at the relationships around you, how many people use heart-tripping, head-tripping or crotch-tripping as a way to create separation? Perhaps you have done it yourself in previous relationships.

It takes a level of courage to get out of this practice. You have to be vulnerable and push all of your barriers down and be honest with yourself. What have you decided that heart-tripping will create for you? What have you decided that head-tripping will create for you? What have you decided that crotch-tripping will create for you?

When I got that heart-tripping wasn't going to create total communion, I started being vigilant and catching myself every time I did it. It is a muscle you have to build. Every single day, any moment that I was heart-tripping, I destroyed and uncreated it and asked for a different reality because what I desire is total awareness and total consciousness in relationship and in my entire life.

Brendon

One of the things that I love about Simone is that whenever she found herself heart-tripping, she caught herself. Sometimes it took a little nudge from me, yet she grabbed it every time. She pulled herself up and worked hard until she changed it. It was awesome. Anything is changeable. As long as you don't buy into whatever is going on for the other person and you don't resist it, that gives them the space to change things much more quickly.

Chapter 9 Tools

- What have you decided that heart-tripping will create for you?
- What have you decided that head-tripping will create for you?
- What have you decided that crotch-tripping will create for you?

'Anything is changeable.'

Brendon

PART TWO
CREATING A PHENOMENAL RELATIONSHIP THAT WORKS FOR YOU

CHAPTER 10

I am single — is that wrong?

Simone

Being single is not wrong. It is not bad, evil and awful.

When I was single and living by myself at Peregian Beach, Queensland, I absolutely loved it. At one stage I was thinking about buying an investment property and renovating it. Now, I am definitely not a handy woman! I remember sitting in my town-house and thinking, 'I could do one of two things. I could either buy a house that is fully renovated, or I could find somebody else who would do that for me.'

I didn't have the sense that something was missing in my life because I didn't have a partner who was a handyman.

One of the questions that Brendon and I get asked by people who say that they desire a relationship yet can't find anyone or even get asked out on a date, is, *what are they doing wrong?*

If you are single and desire a relationship and it seems to elude you — you are going to hate this — that is usually because you don't desire one.

Relationship is not a fairy tale. It is the furthest thing from a fairy tale in the world. There is no knight in shining armour, nor the perfect six-foot blonde who is skinny and tanned all year round.

Brendon doesn't ride a white horse. He owns a grey speckled horse and a tan horse. That doesn't quite fit the picture of a knight in shining armour, although when I look at him on a horse, he *is* my knight in shining armour.

If you truly desire to create a relationship, the first thing to look at is, what does it mean to you? Does it get you out of something? Does it get you into something? Does it save you? Does it create limitation? Does it create contraction? Be willing to have a look at what is real and true for you in every moment.

I definitely had the point of view that relationships were not joyful. I didn't see any great ones, so why would I choose it? The day I changed my point of view on relationships, is also the day Brendon walked into my life.

So the first step is letting go of all the decisions you have made about relationship. For any woman who is reading this, if you have decided that some-one will come along and take care of you and give you a house, and wine and dine you, be prepared to let that go. Why? Every decision limits what can show up. You are trying to order a pre-planned rela-tionship into place rather than receiving the infinite possibilities that are available.

Would you be willing to have a man come into your life for *you* to take care of? What if he had no mon-ey and you were the cash cow? And you paid him for sex. Are you willing to have that and choose that? Because there is no right choice.

Brendon is 11 years younger than I am and this re-ality would call that a toy boy. We did too and had a lot of fun with it. At one stage, Brendon actually Googled the words 'toy boy' and later said to me, 'Do you know what a toy boy's job is? To look good and spend a lot of money!' We laughed because that was what was occurring at one stage in our lives.

THE LIES OF RELATIONSHIP

Brendon

As men, our fathers teach us about relationship but most of them aren't very good at it themselves.

Some men have fathers who teach them to treat women with regard; mine didn't. I used to watch the way my dad acted and think, 'How could you treat people like that?' Luckily for me, I always had a level of regard for others, so I didn't buy the lie that my dad was perpetrating.

Lies are a big topic in any relationship. I am not talking about the lies you tell your partner or the lies they tell you. Nor am I talking about the secrets you keep from them. This is about the lies that you have bought from everyone in your life to create your viewpoints on relationship.

Why do I say that? Because as children, we were not taught to discover what is true for us with relationships, with money or any other aspect of living. I will give you an example. When I was growing up, if I showed any kindness or caring to others, my dad used to tell me, 'You are such a girl. You are such a poofter; you won't be tough.' So I figured that in order to be a man, I had to be rough and tough.

I was also told, 'You have to work hard for money.' So, at 17 I got a job and worked my ass off to earn not much money, because I thought that was true.

The problem is, the people we look to for guidance have based *their* points of view on the lies of others. So from day one, we use lies in order to create our points of view. Since our point of view creates our reality and we have based it on lies, then maybe this whole reality is based on lies!

There are lies in every area of life: with money, sex, relationship, business, family, kids, partners — with everything. If you are stuck or have a problem in any area of your life, there is usually some lie in place.

Lies can be a subtle way of abusing yourself. When you base your choices on lies, you don't look for the greatness you are, and you don't recognise that you are the source of your life. You are not your lies. You are not your agendas. You are *you*.

Choosing for you begins with asking yourself, 'What do I know? What is true for me?'

My relationship with Simone works because I will not give up my point of view for hers and she will not give up her point of view for mine. She does not expect me to cut off parts of me for her. We haven't gone into this relationship with the idea that it has made us whole and now that we are together, we are one.

Please don't go into a relationship with the idea that you are going to be one — that is another lie.

Recognise also that just because you bought a lie or decided to function from lies, it doesn't have to be permanent. Some things have come up for me lately where I had not seen the lie for seven years, yet it was as plain as kangaroo balls to everyone else! As soon as I spotted the lie, I was able to change things.

You can change anything in a heartbeat if you are willing to look at what is limiting your life and where things aren't working. Be honest with yourself and you will change them.

CONGRUENCY IS HOW THINGS GO TOGETHER

Simone

As I said before, if you are not in a relationship right now that is because you do not want one. Maybe you have been trying to appease your family by appearing to choose a relationship, when in reality you are having a good time, travelling the world, doing whatever you choose and you don't have to cook dinner for two.

This is where you have to be honest with yourself because in order to create a relationship, you must be congruent with what you are asking for. What is congruency? As an example, let's say you are asking to have more money in your life. Then you go out to dinner and see a very nice wine that you would like to drink but instantly think you cannot afford it. In that split-second you have un-invited money. This is not about having to buy the most expensive wine every time you go out. It is about recognising that every thought, feeling, and emotion that something is not possible are the lies upon which you have based your life.

Being congruent with what you are asking for is coming out of the lies of impossibility. Is it true you can't afford an expensive bottle of wine? Maybe not today, another day you probably could.

When you are energetically congruent with what you are asking for, there is a natural enthusiasm in your world. You are so inviting that people are drawn to you irresistibly and desire to gift everything to you. This is very easy to see with children. When Nash is being himself, I desire to give him the world; nothing is a limit. When he is not being himself, or acting like a surly teenager, I don't desire to give him anything. His level of receiving is not congruent with what I am willing to gift him.

Congruency is how things go together. When you are happy, you are congruent with your life and living. You go out and get to work to create everything you desire. For instance, when I wanted to go overseas for the first time, I got three jobs. One of my jobs was working in a bar on the weekends so I wouldn't go out with my friends and spend money *in* bars. I desired to travel and getting three jobs was congruent with that desire.

If you say you would love to create a relationship, don't sit back and do nothing because the universe doesn't have any limitation. You do. If you ask for a relationship, the universe will open all the doors that will allow it to occur. Then, you walk along slamming them shut and saying, 'No, no, no! Maybe I will walk through that door in five years' time.'

If you are sincere about creating a relationship, what action could you take today? Perhaps you could go out on a date or go somewhere new so that you could meet a fun and interesting man or woman. After all, what is the worst thing that could happen? If you took some action steps today towards having what you would like as your life and living, in relationships and sex, the worst thing might be that you stumble and fall and have to get back up again. Okay, fine. What if that is the adventure of living?

ASKING FOR A PLAYMATE

Brendon

So, let's talk about dating. The first thing to look at with someone whom you would like to date is, will they be fun? Please start asking yourself that question. And, if you become aware that, no, they won't be fun, don't ask any other questions. Move on. You don't have to go there and prove your awareness is right. Yet so many people do this.

If you ask, 'Will this be fun?' and you get a sense of lightness that is like 'Yes!' and you are looking for someone to play with, then go on the date and enjoy yourself.

If the question you are *really* asking is, 'Will they be fun and will I get a ring on my finger? Will they be fun and how long until I can get them doing everything I want? How long until I can mould them into the person that they should be? How long until they treat me like the princess that I am? How long...?' you have already ruined every single future possibility with that person by all your projections and expectations.

What if dating is about finding somebody who is actually fun to be with? And not about looking for a prison guard for your life. A prison guard is someone you believe you need to control your life, or so you can control their life.

A playmate is literally someone you can look at and ask, 'Want to play?' Does that bring up a sense of playfulness and excitement in your world? Take that into your date because dating should be about enjoyment. Living should be about having fun. Sex should be about having fun, yet we act all serious and worry about, 'What do they want me to look like? What do they want me to be like?' My advice is: be yourself. If they are smart, they will enjoy the hell out of you. If they run away, you don't want them anyway.

....

Let's say you have so much fun on your date that you want to go to bed with them afterwards. Don't stop asking questions. You could ask, 'Will I be happy afterwards? Will I learn something? Will they be grateful?'

What if sex is like playing with a frisbee? You can throw it once, or throw it 500 times until you fall over, as long as it is fun.

Often people will decide what the sex should be like and by the time they actually go to bed, they are so caught up in what they need to do they are not present with their lover. How many people are present during sex? If you are willing to have no point of view about sex, you can be totally present with what is occurring and receive something different from it. Sex is actually about receiving, so the more fun sex you have, the more money you will make and everything will get easier in your life.

Now, if you are in a relationship or dating someone who checks out during sex, that is not necessarily a wrongness. Most probably, they were not taught how, so look for ways to get them present. You might have to tie them up and tickle them with a feather. Don't say out loud to a man, 'What is it going to take for you to be present?' They will make themselves wrong and you will lose them. Ladies, my main tool here is, shut up.

Chapter 10 Tools

- If you are sincere about creating a relationship, look at what action you could take today. Perhaps you could go somewhere new or go out on a date.

- Before going on a date with someone ask yourself, will this be fun? If you become aware that they won't be fun, move on.

'The universe doesn't have any limitation; you do.'

Simone

'Choosing for you begins with asking yourself: What do I know? What is true for me?'

Brendon

CHAPTER 11

Intimacy

Simone

We often misidentify intimacy as getting naked and having sex. Sex is a small part of relationship and don't get me wrong — it is a great part — and it is not intimacy. Your choice to be intimate is what creates intimacy.

You can't have intimacy with someone else until you have intimacy with you and this is easier than you imagine. At the start, I mentioned the five elements for creating intimacy. They are vulnerability, allowance, gratitude, honour and trust.

When I first found out about them in an Access class, I wrote them all down on post-it notes and put them on my bathroom mirror. At the end of each day, I looked at all the places where I had not chosen vulnerability, allowance, gratitude, honour and trust with myself. I didn't think about it much or judge myself for not getting it right that day; I simply destroyed and uncreated it. That is how I began creating a greater sense of intimacy with me.

For Brendon and I, intimacy is the daily choice to have these five elements with ourselves and also with each other. Every choice we make is an honouring of ourselves and the other person.

Vulnerability, allowance, gratitude, honour and trust are not always what we think they are. For instance, vulnerability is usually considered a weakness. So many of us have grown up with our dukes up ready to protect ourselves, or else we build walls to keep us safe. These walls must be made of some indestructible material because no one and nothing can get past them!

In a relationship you have to be vulnerable and be aware of every single choice you make and every choice the other person makes. Vulnerability is not weakness. It is a huge strength. It is like being a marshmallow; you poke a marshmallow and what happens? It just bounces back.

When you are vulnerable you can't be destroyed because you will always know what works for you and you have true choice in every aspect of your life.

Brendon

Growing up, I definitely thought it was wrong to be vulnerable.

Has anyone ever told you, 'If you do that you will be vulnerable'? It means opening yourself up to outside things that can hurt you. Even a brick wall can be vulnerable. If you remove a particular brick it could weaken the whole wall.

This was rather confusing for me because as a boy I found it very easy to be vulnerable and rather challenging too. When you have *no* walls or barriers to anything, you receive everything that is going on around you.

I clearly remember one particular day, I must have been about six years old at the time, I was at school, just sitting under a tree and bawling my eyes out. Until that point there hadn't been a single day in my life when I didn't cry about something. I perceived the enormous sadness in the world, and since no one had told me otherwise, I thought I was the sad one.

That day at school I decided to stop being vulnerable and start fitting in with everyone else, because otherwise it would get too hard. I spent the next 24 years perfecting the art of fitting in, which didn't work for me either.

After going to several Access Consciousness classes, I looked at the energy of vulnerability again. I noticed the places in my life where I was putting up walls to things and realised it would be a whole lot easier to receive different people, situations, or energies if I didn't have any barriers to them.

We don't just build walls; we build fortresses around us! They are supposedly there to keep us safe, yet we actually keep ourselves in. The idea of needing protection from anything is a lie. As an infinite being, would you need protection from anything? From anyone?

Being vulnerable is like being a rock in the stream; everything goes around you and nothing ever affects you. You have no walls or barriers to anything, including you.

Nowadays when things come up that I don't want to look at, or seem hard to deal with, I find them much easier to change from a place of vulnerability. I do my best to put up no barriers to anything, and in that, I receive a whole lot more information because when you are vulnerable the universe will gift you everything.

Vulnerability is the willingness to acknowledge you are not perfect — and you don't need to be. It is the realisation that you have got some really cool stuff going on and some not-so-cool stuff going on. You don't hide from anyone and anything. Most of all you don't hide the brilliance of you. We always think that what we hide the most is our pettiness or anger. The truth is that most often behind the anger and the smallness, we hide our brilliance.

BEING YOURSELF NO MATTER WHAT

Simone

Vulnerability is also looking at anything that comes up for you without having to bottle things up or put on a brave face, even if this makes you uncomfortable.

During the first 18 months of our relationship, one day I went for a walk on the beach and started looking at my life: what I thought I wanted to create and what actually was being created.

When I came back home, I went into the bedroom and sat on my bed and started crying. Brendon came in and sat on the chair next to me and asked, 'Hey, what's up?'

'I don't know if I can do this,' I replied.

'What do you mean? Do what?' he asked.

At that time we were living in a two-bedroom town-house where previously I had lived on my own. The second bedroom was my office. It had a fold-out sofa and that's what Nash was sleeping on most nights. We didn't have the dog yet! He came later.

I said to Brendon, 'I didn't ever think that I would have a child and now I have got this five-year old around all the time.'

He looked at me and said, 'Well, I sort of come with a five-year-old.'

As soon as he said that, I got it. He was right.

Brendon added, 'We don't have to do this relationship like this. I could move out. It doesn't mean we would have to break up. It just means it will look different because we won't be living together any-more. What would *you* like?'

I was so grateful that he was willing to ask what would work for me. He didn't give me an ultimatum or present me with an either/or scenario because it never is an either/or universe.

In relationship, you have to get that you have choice and you have to keep asking yourself every day: *what is it you truly desire to create?* You must have that. It is imperative. You cannot get lost in somebody else's reality. You have to know what *you* truly desire to create.

After this conversation, I started to play with different scenarios of what I would like and desire in my life. Not long after that conversation, Brendon went up north in Queensland to do some work, which gave me the space to look at what I would like to have and create in my life.

One night while he was away I went to an Access Bars® swap. That is where people who have learned to do the Bars get together to swap this body process with each other. Nash had been staying with his grandma during this time and both of them showed up to the Bars swap. When Nash came in the door, he ran up to me and gave me the biggest hug. He looked at me with those big, beautiful eyes and told me how much he loved me. Later on that evening, while he was running around with the other children, he fell over and grazed his knee. I was having my Bars run at the time but he came to me for help. He cuddled into me as I lay on the massage table and didn't look to his grandma for anything!

I later realised that Nash was smart. Perhaps not cognitively, yet somewhere in his world he knew that if he wanted to create the life he desired, I matched the energy of what he desired in his life too.

When I went home that night, I looked at the energy that Nash is and the contribution he is to my life. I never dreamed I would have children; I never desired to have children. Yet when I looked at the energy Nash was being with me and what a contribution that was, I also didn't desire to *not* have that energy in my life.

That was definitely a turning point for me. It was a different level of commitment to Brendon and to Nash. Since he was going to be in my life, I also looked at what I was to him? I never said to Nash, 'I am your mum.' Instead I asked him, 'What would you like me to be for *you*?'

Over the years, I have periodically asked him this question. Whenever we hit a rough patch I will ask, 'OK, Nash, what would you like me to be for you? I can be that.'

We have had some great conversations over the years. Now he is a teenager, so we will see what is next on the path.

I share this story to show you that there are moments like this in life that are uncomfortable. If you are willing to be yourself no matter what it takes, and not put up walls and barriers, then what shows up is always greater.

Vulnerability is a huge strength in any relationship, even in a business relationship. I see so many people defend themselves when there is a problem rather than admitting they were wrong. It takes vulnerability to tell someone with sincerity, 'I was being such an asshole; I am really sorry. What can I do to make up for the damage done?'

Admitting that you acted like a bitch, or an asshole, is disarming and it will create far greater possibilities than judging yourself or fighting to prove that you are right. So, if you have created some crap in your life, be vulnerable enough to admit it to yourself. 'Yes, I have created some crap, now what would I like to choose? What would I like to add to my life?'

You making that demand of yourself will change whatever is going on and you don't have to do it all by yourself. You can request help of the universe. You can literally say, 'Hey universe, help me out here.'

What would you rather choose? Getting drunk and complaining about your relationship or making a demand of yourself to be the five elements of intimacy? You can choose the first option if you like.

Just recognise that that choice will not create the change that you desire.

Chapter 11 Tools

- Vulnerability is looking at whatever comes up for you without having to bottle things up or put on a brave face, even if this makes you un-comfortable.

- A question to ask yourself daily: *'What is it I tru-ly desire to create as my life?'*

'Creating a great relationship requires a level of intimacy that very few people are willing to have even with themselves, let alone someone else.'

Simone

CHAPTER 12

The key of allowance

Brendon

There is this romantic notion that being in a relationship means you are one. Relationship is not that you are one. Relationship is, 'You are here; I am here. What can we create together that is greater than what we can create apart?'

If Simone wakes up funky one morning, or is dealing with something, I don't try and fix things for her, even though a man's job is to fix. From an early age most little boys are taught by their mothers to do things for women. They will say things like, 'Would you do this for mummy?' and as men we take on the role of fixing.

But I have realised that being invasive in Simone's world doesn't work. What works is being in allowance of her choices and letting her know, 'Hey, I get that you are cranky right now and if you require anything I am over here. Just ask.'

Allowance is a huge part of creating a generative relationship. When you allow the other person to choose whatever they choose, you don't have to make them right or make *you* wrong for anything. You don't have to judge their choices as good or bad. At the same time you don't let them walk over you, because allowance is not being a doormat.

It is having no point of view except that everything is an interesting point of view. You can literally say, 'Interesting point of view I am choosing to be cranky today,' or 'Interesting point of view Simone is choosing to be cranky today,' or whatever is going on in that moment.

I always found it easy to have allowance for other people. When it came to having allowance for myself, it was a different story because I did not always like myself. Simone, all my friends and the people around me kept saying, 'Brendon, you are so amazing; you are so kind and caring.' I thought they were a bunch of nut jobs!

After a while, I began wondering what they saw in me that I was not willing to see. I started to look at myself through their eyes. Gradually, I began to recognise all the things I had done throughout my life, the caring I had for people and the kindness I had shown in different situations. Holy shit! That was when I started to look at who I actually am, and not who I judged myself to be. Please know that it didn't happen overnight; I worked my butt off.

Another thing that helped me to get out of self-judgement was to enjoy it. Whenever I noticed myself starting to judge something I said or did, I would say, 'Wow, I am judging myself harshly right now. This is awesome. This is hilarious! I would choose this for what reason?' It went from being serious and significant to being a bit of a joke.

THE GIFT OF EACH OTHER'S PRESENCE

Simone

Brendon has changed a lot. All the same, I remember the time when for three days at a stretch he didn't do anything except mope around all day. Now, I am one of those people who wakes up with a huge amount of energy every morning. I might go for a run or hop on my computer and start my day.

Even though Brendon was sad for three whole days, I didn't try to cheer him up or think that his sadness was my fault. I just kept creating and doing my thing. On the third day, he looked at me and said, 'Would you stop being so happy?'

I said, 'No.'

Then we both started laughing because Brendon had nowhere to go with that. I was allowing him to choose the mood he was in and I wasn't buying into it. Eventually, he himself realised that being sad every day of his life, while I was walking around being happy, was not much fun.

Be aware that allowance is not always smooth sailing.

Allowance is chaos and chaos is allowance. Let me give you another example. As I mentioned in a previous chapter, Brendon is our CFO (Chief Financial Officer) and he also runs our stock portfolio. He includes me in it and yet he is the one who buys and sells shares of his own accord, based on his awareness. There are times when he will say, 'Hey let's have a chat about something.' Usually, over a glass of wine, or in a taxi on the way to a restaurant, we will talk about a stock and just get each other's awareness on it. Yet I allow him to make his choices based on what he knows. If something seems funky in my world about a certain stock I will say to Brendon, 'This is a little strange...'

I remember a time when this couple, good friends of ours, were in New York. She had just taken over as the CFO of their relationship and, while buying and selling stock one day, she lost $50,000 in 30 seconds.

Her husband's response was, 'Oh well, darling. What else is possible and how does it get any better than that?'

He knew that he had to be in total allowance of what had just occurred, otherwise his wife would start judging the choices she made. He also realised that, 'Guess what? She could make $50,000 in 30 seconds, too.'

This enabled him to be in total allowance of her choices and in allowance of himself for handing over the reins of their stock portfolio to her.

True intimacy is having allowance for the other person and every single thing they choose, even if it may seem like a mistake. How many people are willing to have that in their relationship?

The number of women who talk about changing their partners, or trying to get them to do something different, astounds me. Ladies, that is not your job! The man in your life didn't ask you to come along and change them into what you have decided is the perfect man for you.

The man, or woman, who is in front of you, can be a gift in your life. One of my favourite times of the day is jumping in bed with Brendon. I love sleeping next to him and it is not about the sex. I get to wake up next to him in the morning, I can touch him, and it is a gift to just be in each other's presence.

There was one morning when we had to get up at 5:30 for some reason. I woke up first and when I heard Brendon stirring, I went into the room and asked him, 'Do you want to wake up with a wristy?' (If you don't know what a 'wristy' is, it is called a hand job in America.)

Brendon's response was, 'I had the strangest dreams last night.'

So, I put my hand on his chest gently, like saying, 'hey', and showing him the energy of him. Then I asked if he would like a coffee. He said, 'Yeah, that would be great.'

To me there was no difference between offering to give him a wristy or make a cup of coffee. Both were done from kindness and the gratitude I have for him in my life. I made neither coffee nor copulation significant and this is one of the things that makes our relationship so different.

You could easily imagine a different scenario. Scenario two could have been me saying, 'How come you don't want to have sex with me?' I could have just gone crazy. Except, why would I choose that?

In that moment as he was waking up, I received him in totality and he received me in totality. There was nothing significant about any of it. We didn't make either of us right or wrong. We had total allowance for, and no judgement of, each other.

There is an Access tool called living in 10-seconds that we use. It is about living in the energy of constant creation. You don't cognitively know what is going to show up next in life, yet each and every moment you create the energy that will create a future which adds to your life and contributes to your life and does not contract or detract from it.

If you don't have allowance in your current relationship, then look at what you are choosing. This is where you need to be brutally honest with yourself. It is not about having coffee with your friends and complaining, 'Oh my god, if he changed this and this, things would be so much better.' Because you always have the choice to stay in the relationship.

If you are single and desire a relationship, start to look at the energy you would like to invite into your life. You can do what I did and ask for someone who is kind, caring, nurturing *and* willing to create with you.

In the past, kindness and caring were not things I looked for in a relationship. It seemed so wishy washy. Then I realised that kindness and caring is not about someone hugging you constantly and telling you how fantastic you are. Someone who is kind, caring and nurturing will allow you to be *you* no matter what occurs. Someone who is kind and caring will also tell you when you are being an asshole. They are willing to be in allowance of what you choose, without being a doormat.

One of my favourite things about Brendon is that he does not align with my point of view and agree with me when I am acting crazy, resisting something or not being willing to choose something. He will ask me a question and then allow me to choose something different or not.

Chapter 12 Tools

- True intimacy is allowing the other person to choose whatever they choose even if it seems like a mistake to you.

- If you are single and desire a relationship, ask for someone who is kind, caring, nurturing *and* willing to create with you.

'Ladies, the man in your life didn't ask you to come along and change him into what you have decided is the perfect man for you.'

Simone

CHAPTER 13

Living in gratitude

Simone

Not long after I first met Gary Douglas, I went to a seminar he was presenting on relationships. That was quite some years ago, and I am still grateful to Gary because that was the first time I didn't feel wrong for not choosing to be in a relationship and not wanting to get married and have kids. I realised that I could create my life from the sense of adventure that had always appealed to me.

Life cannot be an adventure when you judge everything as being wrong or right; that is about being in control. To have the adventure of living from the infinite possibilities that are available requires a level of gratitude that few people have. When you have gratitude, you will look for the awareness in everything that occurs in your life, the successes and the setbacks. As your gratitude increases, everything becomes an inclusion to greater possibility.

I was talking with Gary about gratitude one day and here is what he said, 'Gratitude is that place of recognising that each and everything in life contributes to you. Gratitude is never shutting off your receiving, so you have the awareness of what you are grateful for, that will create more in life.'

From gratitude, everything grows and expands. Yet we have never been taught to be grateful for every single thing in life — the good, the unpleasant and the awful. It is not easy to be grateful when things aren't going your way. For instance, let's take money. How often are you grateful for money? Or do you go into judgement about the money you don't have? Do you go into judgement about the amount of money you would like to have? Whether you have money in your bank account or not, be grateful for it and know that there is no limit to the amount of money you can invite into your life. Limitation cannot exist simultaneously with gratitude. Judgement cannot exist simultaneously with gratitude.

When you judge the people in your life, be they your partner, your children or even the people with whom you work, you stop seeing them as valuable. If you have gratitude for them, you begin to see their value in ways you have not been willing to recognise before. The purpose of gratitude is to increase your awareness. And when your awareness increases, so do your money flows. For me, the more I was grateful for Brendon, the more money he made and the more money I made. It is not linear; money never is!

Research has found that when someone talks to a plant and is grateful for it and treats it with admiration, that plant grows more rapidly. If someone yells at their plant and abuses it, it starts to contract and die. That is what you are doing by yelling at yourself for perceived failings, the things you haven't created and the money you haven't made. Judgement always contracts your energy and kills all your future possibilities.

What if every single day, even if you brought in no money, you gave yourself a high five and said, 'Yeah! I'm the best.' Or send yourself the 'You Rock' emoticon. Doesn't that seem like more fun than sitting in judgement of you for being bad and wrong for not making much money?

A question that Brendon and I ask every day is: what revenue streams can we create and what can we add to our lives?

Then we go about our day, because we don't have a set idea about what these revenue streams are going to look like. It is not about writing a to-do list. When we become aware of an energy that is inviting us to a different possibility, we will take action.

We keep choosing and moving forward and keep following the energy of adventure which allows us to create way more than before. And we have gratitude for every choice we make, even the so-called mistakes.

RANDOM ACTS OF GRATITUDE

I know that I can be quite intense and full on. I go at 100 miles an hour and yet Brendon loves living with me. He is willing for me to be me and I am willing for him to be him.

Are you grateful for the man or woman in your life and what you are creating together?

When you are grateful for what you are creating, amazing things show up; random acts of gratitude show up. I remember one occasion where I was sweating over something and Brendon said, 'I wish you could see how great you are. I wish you could see how great you are through my eyes.'

Being totally vulnerable and receiving gratitude from others is not always comfortable, and it is a choice that can transform your life and transform your relationship.

WHAT IF THERE IS NOTHING WRONG WITH YOUR RELATIONSHIP?

Brendon

If you have gratitude for you, you will never judge you. If you have gratitude for your partner, you will never judge them.

People in relationship like to talk about what's wrong with their relationship. What I say is, 'There is never anything wrong with your relationship. There is only what you are unwilling to choose.'

To be honest, I came into this relationship thinking it was going to be hard work. Until that point, my whole life had been about how hard everything is and how you have to struggle to succeed.

For 30 years of my life I thought that all the sadness and unhappiness I perceived was mine. I was convinced that I was sad, unhappy and depressed. It took me two or three years of asking, 'Who does this belong to?' non-stop every time sadness came up, before things changed. Eventually, I got to a point where it was easier to be aware of energies. Right now, I could perceive sadness and I know it is not mine. It doesn't go away necessarily when I ask, 'Who does this belong to?' yet I am now aware of my reality and have a sense of who I am.

Simone is quite the opposite. She wakes up every morning excited to create and in my head I used to think, 'Why are you so happy? I just want to go back to sleep.'

You know the saying, 'Don't judge someone until you have walked a mile in their shoes'? I will always be grateful that she didn't judge me. She gave me the space to discover for myself the life I wished to create.

Simone was willing to see who I was, way before I did. She would say things like, 'You are a great guy; you are so amazing.' That was *not* how I saw myself at the time.

When we met I had zero dollars in the bank, or let's say I was in the red a lot. She could have kicked me out. She could have said, 'Get to work.' She saw in me what I could create that I was not yet creating and she was always there for me. I am grateful that she always has my back.

One of the things I am grateful for is, if one of us is exhausted or has something going on, the other person does not have to fix it. That doesn't mean we ignore the other person and leave them to suffer! We will look at what we could contribute to help them out. Could I run Simone's Bars or do something else?

There was one point when I was having a hard time. I had hit my crank capacity. It had never got that bad, ever.

Simone said, 'Do you want to go away somewhere for a couple of days on your own and I will take Nash?' I was so grateful for that. I had no desire to do it because my life is much easier when I am around her, yet having the freedom to choose helped me a lot.

Gratitude is a tool you can use in your relationship right away. Every day look at the person you are in relationship with and ask yourself: 'What is the one thing about them that I am most grateful for?' Your relationship will always expand because gratitude has that energy of expansion.

THE WAY WE HAVE BEEN DOING RELATIONSHIP DOESN'T WORK

Simone

One of the things that occurs when you function from gratitude is that your capacity to receive will increase. This does not mean everything will be joyous in every moment of the day. There are moments in life that are not always as easy as you would like them to be.

In relationship there will be times when you have an upset and Brendon and I have that too. We don't say, 'We have got this.' We use the tools and some of them are not that easy to use.

One day I was upset with Brendon about something, I can't remember what it was about exactly. As I said before we live across from the beach, so I went for a walk to clear my head. Just at that moment Gary called me. He picked up straight away that I was upset and the first thing he said was, 'What's up?'

I said, 'I'm cranky at Brendon...'

Gary said, 'You need to go home and make it all about him.'

That was the last thing in the world I wanted to do. Since I knew the Access tools worked for everything else, I went home and did exactly what Gary had suggested. Within 10 minutes, I am not kidding, Brendon was saying, 'Honey, can I get you a drink? Would you like a Bloody Mary? What can I make you for dinner tonight?'

I remember sitting on the couch and thinking, 'Seriously? This shit really works!'

This tool is sometimes still hard for me to use, and, if I notice something is not as creative with Brendon as I would like, I will use it. Because this relationship didn't just happen. We created it by using the tools and by our choices.

If someone is being an asshole, they are either just an asshole, or there is something they require that they are not getting. Use the tool of making it all about them. You can copy what women did in the 1950s. When your man comes home, pour him a whisky. Cook him dinner and acknowledge him. Take him into the bedroom or have a shower with him. Make it all about him and see what changes in your relationship.

This tool, like all Access Consciousness® tools, is about you having more choice and more aware-ness so that you can choose something different. In truth, the way we have been doing relationship just doesn't work for a lot of people. Einstein's defi-nition of insanity is doing the same thing over and over and expecting a different result. What if we did something totally different? What if you creat-ed a relationship that is totally unconventional?

In a conventional relationship, the good times are the holidays and the sex and the bad times are the fighting, arguing and make-up sex. I am sorry. There is no way in the world I would ever be inter-ested in make-up sex and I know Brendon wouldn't be either.

Chapter 13 Tools

- Practise gratitude for your partner. It will increase your awareness and when your awareness increases, so do your money flows. The more Simone was grateful for Brendon, the more money he made and the more money she made.

- A question to ask every day: what revenue streams can you create and what can you add to your life?

If you have gratitude for you, you will never judge you. If you have gratitude for your partner, you will never judge them.'

Brendon Watt

CHAPTER 14

Do you trust me?

Simone

If you have ever been in a relationship where there was very little honouring or trust, then you will know it is not pleasant or generative.

In the past I have chosen some horrible relationships. There was one particular relationship where I used to wake up crying every morning — and I thought that was normal. He wasn't physically abusive; he constantly put me down and made me think that I was unworthy, which matched my judgement of myself at the time.

Now, this man and I were housemates. After he broke up with me, he hooked up with another girl and used to have sex with her in the room across from mine. I could clearly hear them. Because I thought I was still in love with him, I thought I must have done something wrong. That level of unkindness towards someone is not only unacceptable;

it is totally dishonouring of them. Being willing to honour yourself and the other person is a big step in making a relationship work.

To honour is to treat someone with regard and to not disregard anybody. When you treat someone with regard you look into their world and see who they are. You recognise what they desire in every moment. You see what they can receive, what they think is important, yet you don't push them in the direction you would like them to go. You allow them to choose for themselves.

When I first hooked up with Brendon, Gary told me: 'You need to let Brendon create his life; you need to stay out of it. Don't get involved.'

Anyone who knows me knows that when I get involved in something I tend to take over!

Brendon is a terrific dad. There are so many ways that he can empower other parents so they have ease with parenting. If I had insisted that he do things my way, I would not be honouring of his choices. So for the first three years, whenever Brendon came up with an idea, I allowed him to create it his way and I was always available to talk about anything.

Sometimes, just having a conversation where you are in total allowance of the other person and listening to what they are creating is a massive contribution to them and a huge contribution to your relationship.

For example, you could ask questions of your partner about what they are creating such as, 'Is that fun for you? Does it make you lighter?'

Don't tell them, 'I think you should do this and that,' which is how so many people function in relationship. When you try to determine what somebody should choose based on your points of view, you are actually disregarding them and what they can choose.

Making a choice to honour you is not always doing the popular thing. I remember one particular day when I woke up in a huge funk. Now Brendon, Nash and I were all going to the same Access class that day in Noosa, on Queensland's Sunshine Coast.

How do you honour everyone, the whole household, when you don't want to be involved with anything?

Then I realised something: we have two cars! Driving on my own while listening to very loud music was more expansive for me and for them, rather than getting in a car with Brendon and Nash, and still being funky. So that is what I did.

For a lot of people, being in relationship means having to do everything together and having to be together all the time. No. Being able to choose *what* you want to choose *when* you want to choose it, is actually one of the most inclusionary things you can do in a relationship. Then every choice you make is a constant contribution to the other person and your child. That is how you create a relationship that actually works for you.

Brendon

Honour is also the willingness to have regard for you, which means that you recognise the gift you are for *you*. Not the gift you are for everyone else. For you! And you don't make yourself small in the face of anyone or sell yourself short. How many people go into relationship based on how somebody looks, or what they think they have, rather than who they are? Just because somebody is in a pretty package, or has a nice figure, doesn't mean anything. What interests me is who they are as a being and what they can contribute.

We all have different capacities. We are all great in our own ways, yet very often we look at ourselves through other people's points of view, which are usually based on lies.

If you truly desire a relationship that is going to work, you cannot go into it expecting the other person to validate you for anything. You have to know the value of you. Even if no one else does it, be willing to acknowledge yourself. Don't wait for anyone else to do it. Because if you are looking for someone else to validate you for something, you have already decided that you are inferior.

Our relationship works so well because Simone is willing to honour herself and she is willing to honour me. Honouring has a sense of longevity to it. When you treat someone with regard in every moment, that builds up over the years because every day is different. What is honouring of Simone today will be different tomorrow. It will constantly change as we change and the circumstances of our life change.

TRUST IS NOT OWNERSHIP

Brendon

People talk a lot about trust in relationship. Trust and honour are not ownership. We do not do ownership in our relationship. I do not own Simone; she does not own me. We totally trust each other to choose more, because we always have done so. Even when those choices haven't turned out the way that I thought they would, the choices I have made got me to where I needed to go.

And this is the same for you too. Please acknowledge that you have never made any wrong choices. Maybe you made some choices that seemed very stupid. Yet, all of those choices got you to where you are today.

Have you ever heard someone say, 'I trust them not to cheat on me'? That is not trust; that is having blind faith in the other person and it does not work. The instant you trust that your partner is always going to do the right thing, you have shut off your awareness.

I was talking with a lady recently who kept getting in relationships with men who would later cheat on her. I suggested that *before* she got into any relationship she ask some questions about them: 'Is this guy going to cheat on me? Yes? No?'

This is a tool you can use as well. If, after asking those questions, you realise they will cheat on you, don't even go there. It is too much fucking work. And, if you are in a relationship where they did cheat on you, please acknowledge that it is not because you are bad or wrong. They cheated on you because they have decided that they are not good enough or they need something else.

Simone

Trust is not what you think it is. In the beginning both Brendon and I trusted that the other person was going to be mean and abusive and leave the relationship. Now, I trust that Brendon will always choose what is going to be greater for him, even if that means going off and finding another woman. That is a rather extreme example, because I know he wouldn't deliberately cheat or do something to hurt me. If his life is moving forward and he found something greater, I trust that he would choose that and wouldn't give himself up to remain in a relationship with me.

Sometimes in our seminars, people will ask us questions about having sex with other people while already in a relationship. Personally, I have never desired it. I love having sex with Brendon and that is the choice I choose every day. I do trust that if he did it, it wouldn't be about cheating on me. It would not be done against me, rather as an expansion of him. That is why relationship has to be a choice every day or you will kill it.

Brendon

We tend to make trust about the other person, it is equally important to trust yourself. If you are willing to trust you, then you will recognise who is a trust-worthy person and who isn't.

Trust of self is knowing that you can handle your life and the situations of your life. You don't function from the need of somebody else or make them the source of your life. When you trust you, even if there are road bumps, you know that you will find your way.

So many people have this idea that once they are in relationship with someone they must hold on to the other person and that is their level of intimacy with them. It might work for the first few weeks, however eventually that needy pull will become a drain on the relationship.

People do *need* in relationship for two common reasons: they have already decided they lack some-thing and are looking for the other person to vali-date who they have decided they can't be, or else they want to hide something.

You will not create intimacy in any relationship that is not about adding to your life in the long run. And like Simone said, if you can't trust yourself, honour yourself, be grateful for and vulnerable with your-self, you can't expect to have that with anyone else.

Chapter 14 Tools

- Be willing to treat yourself and your partner with regard even though it may not be the popular thing to do.

- Trust isn't always about the other person, if you are willing to trust you, then you will recognise who is a trustworthy person and who isn't.

'Trust is not what you think it is. If Brendon's life is moving forward and he found something greater, I trust that he would choose that and wouldn't give himself up to remain in a relationship with me.'

Simone

'Trust and honour are not ownership... I do not own Simone; she does not own me. We totally trust each other to choose more because we always have done so.'

Brendon

CHAPTER 15

Sexy time

Simone

What have you decided that sex has to be that it is not?

I used to think that if you were in a relationship it meant you had sex all the time and that every time you saw each other it was about jumping into bed. Isn't that what they portray in the movies?

One day the unthinkable happened. I wanted to have sex and Brendon didn't. Instead, he said, 'Do you want to go for a walk on the beach and have dinner?'

Immediately after that he said, 'Gross! Did I really say that?'

I replied, 'Yeah, you did.'

We had just started seeing each other and I remember freaking out because if Brendon and I were just hooking up and having sex, I could deal with that. Having somebody in my life who desired to hang out with me because he thought I was amazing and wonderful, that totally spun me out. I had to be vulnerable and see how I was a contribution to him and how he was a contribution to me. That is when Brendon looked at me and said, 'You *do* get this is not just about sex for me, right?'

....

Brendon has a different outlook on sex. He is not like most people who get turned on by judgement. He is one of those rare people who have no judgement in their world. One time he said, 'How often do two people have sex together because they both desire it at the same time? Usually, one person is doing it to please the other.'

I realised that he was right. There were definitely times in our relationship where I asked him for sex and he said, 'Not now, honey.'

It would have been easy to become offended by that, rather than acknowledge that he simply didn't desire to have sex in that moment.

What if every single time you had sex it was different? Brendon has shown me how to have way more ease and fun with sex. It doesn't matter what is going on, or what occurred; we have a sense of play. That is literally what it should be.

If you have someone in your life, you could ask them, 'Do you want to take your clothes off and get naked and play?' That doesn't mean you must have sex; it doesn't mean you must have an orgasm; it doesn't have to last for hours. It doesn't mean anything except: do you want to get naked and play?

SEX AND RELATIONSHIP ARE TWO DIFFERENT THINGS

Brendon

A lot of people use sex to validate who they are. Their reasoning is, if they can pleasure someone then they must be good at sex, or they must be a good person. There are people who use sex to validate the status of their relationship by saying, 'If the sex is good, then the relationship is good.'

Sex and relationship are two completely different things.

Sex is a great part of relationship, yet it isn't everything. What would make it greater is looking at what could you do today to enjoy the hell out of sex with your partner. Rather than deciding what having sex means before you even touch them.

People attach a lot of meaning to sex and that always confused me, even as a young boy. I am a little bit different. For me, sex is something you do for the absolute joy of it. It is no different to playing with a frisbee at the beach. We don't make that significant!

What if we looked at having sex in the same way? It could last 10 minutes. It could last an hour, who cares so long as you are enjoying it? Start enjoying your relationships. Start enjoying sex. What would the enjoyment of sex be like for *you*?

WHAT WOULD PAYING FOR SEX CHANGE FOR YOU?

Simone

During the first 18 months we were together, when I fully supported Brendon while he was figuring out what he wanted to do, he had no money of his own. It is not nice having to ask for $50 to buy a bottle of wine to go with the amazing meal he was cooking us. Also, I didn't want to say, 'Here's $50 for cooking dinner.'

One day, Gary Douglas suggested that I offer to pay Brendon for sex. Now that was not an easy gig for me. I did *not* want to pay for sex! It would mean I was a whore, or that I couldn't get sex without paying for it etc. Millions of excuses and reasons not to do it came up for me. Given how much resistance I had to this idea, I knew going through with it would create dynamic change for me.

I also wanted to empower Brendon to make his own choices with money. I didn't desire for him to rely on me; I desired him to create his life and be as great as I knew he was. So as uncomfortable as it was, I went home and suggested we have sex.

Brendon was busy doing something and he wasn't that interested. That is when I said, 'What if I paid you $500 to have sex?'

His whole body lit up when I said that. And, we had so much fun! The sex was amazing and afterwards, I left the money on the bed side table — we made a joke of it.

What I loved about it was Brendon went out and spent half the money on himself, to have a massage. With the rest of the money, he bought us dinner and some wine. I knew that he felt great about having money and being able to choose to do whatever he wanted to do with it. It was quite an honouring of him and I got over my point of view that paying for sex was bad and wrong. Everyone does it. If you are having sex, you are paying for it in some way. So, if you would like to spice things up in your relationship, you could do that.

JOY AND LAUGHTER DURING SEX

Brendon

What I always say is, have some fun with sex. Act like sex is one big game and not a necessity. Mix it up and make it different. It could be on the kitchen bench. What if you were to ask your man, 'Hey do you want a blow job in the kitchen?' Make it fun for both of you and not something you do on schedule simply because it is Friday night and that is sex time. When it is spontaneous that is usually when you enjoy the hell out of it.

There was one time when Simone wanted to have sex and I didn't want to. The way I see it is, both people should desire to have sex because if I had gone ahead with it, what contribution would that have been to me or to her? I would have given myself up in order to make her happy. Sex is about the interaction between you and the joyful contribution that can be to you and your bodies.

Just because I didn't want sex on that particular day doesn't mean I wouldn't like to be asked another time. So, if you initiate sex with your woman or your man, and they say no, don't make yourself wrong. It doesn't mean you now must wait for the other person to ask you.

What if, sometime later, you simply asked them again? That is what I mean about having fun and play. Ever noticed that when kids want to play they will ask, 'Can we go to the park?' If you say, 'Not now,' they will wait a bit and ask again and again because the next time you just might say, 'Yeah, I would love to go to the park with you.'

How many people actually have joy and laughter during sex?

Sex and copulation have been used as a tool and a weapon in this reality. Some people use copulation in order to prove something about themselves, which means they are already in judgement. Sex without judgement is having no point of view about what it should look like, how long it should go for, who should orgasm first. Those are all judgements. There are a lot of men who require judgement to be turned on because they have learned about sex by looking at porn, or from judgemental people. If they are the people who you like to copulate with, that is fine, just know you have to put a level of judgement into their world so they get turned on.

There are literally thousands and thousands of points of view around sex. Some might be: 'If I have sex with them, I can control them,' Or 'If I have sex with them, then they will stay with me.' What does any of that have to do with fun?

If you desire to have sex from the sheer joy of it here are four questions to ask yourself: 'Will it be fun? Will it be easy? Will I learn something? Will I be happy afterwards?' Every question you ask will give you some energetic awareness. If it is not going to be fun, stop at that question. Don't ask the other three. Sex does not have to be as serious and significant as it is made out to be.

….

Simone

There are studies to show that once people have been married for a while, the number of times a year they have sex diminishes. The longer they stay married, the less sex they have. That is how relationship is done in this reality; it doesn't have to be that way.

If you want to have some fun with sex, the next time you are having dinner with your Enjoyable Other, point out the people around you. When we go out I will often say to Brendon, 'Check out that chick, look at her long legs.'

And, quite often I will be the one to initiate sex because that is what most women do. Most men have been taught that they have to wait until the woman says yes. If a woman says 'No,' the man has to back off. There are women who give off that vibe of 'No, not tonight,' so the man tends not to initiate things.

If things have gone off the boil in the bedroom, start initiating more play. You could just stroke your partner, or give them a nice foot massage. Even if you play with yourself in the shower, or with your partner just do it from the joyful orgasmic energy. It doesn't need to lead to copulation.

Chapter 15 Tools

- Sex does not have to be as serious and significant as most people tend to think. If you desire to have sex from the sheer joy of it there are four questions to ask:
  - » Will it be fun?
  - » Will it be easy?
  - » Will I learn something?
  - » Will I be happy afterwards?

Every question you ask will give you some energetic awareness.

'If you have someone in your life ask them: Do you want to take your clothes off and get naked and play?'

Simone

CHAPTER 16

Sharing is not caring

Simone

Ever noticed that men and women communicate in different ways?

If you desire to have an easier time in relationship, one of the tools is to communicate with your lover, or Enjoyable Other, the way *they* like to communicate. There are different styles of communication for men and for women and neither one is right or wrong. Just using this one tool will make a huge difference in your relationship.

A man's style of communication is usually quite direct. He might say things like, 'Let's do this, this, this, this, this.'

Whereas someone who communicates like a woman generally has to talk things out and share how they feel. This is not something only women do; I definitely know some men who communicate like this also.

To give you an example from the business world, when I deal with people who function more like a man, I know we can get down to brass tacks straight away. So I will say to them, 'Will this work? Okay, let's do this; let's change this.' In business, I definitely communicate more like a man would and we get through things pretty fast.

Then there are other people with whom I deal who have to talk things out more. When I am in a meeting with them, I will start with small talk and allow them to have their say. Usually, something that could be done in 10 minutes, may take at least an hour and I have learned to be in allowance of them. This is not about judging your partner or your work mates. Use this information to gain awareness of how somebody likes to communicate, so you have more clarity and ease of communication in all your relationships, not just your intimate ones.

NEVER SHARE WITH YOUR MAN

Brendon

One of the myths we are told is that for a relationship to be strong, you need to be open with each other and communicate everything. This usually means you need to give someone your point of view and they need to give you theirs. That is a one-way street; it is not communication.

If you are willing to look at your girlfriend, lover or wife from the perspective of, 'What can this person hear and what can this person receive?' — then you will communicate very differently with them. Before you open your mouth to say anything, always ask yourself: what can they hear? Never, ever, tell someone what they cannot hear. If you do, they have to fight you in order to defend themselves.

Another big point to remember with your gentleman, or with your lady, is do not help them unless they ask for it. As soon as you go to help someone, you have already assumed that you know better and you are superior. If you do that to a man, he will, of necessity, put up walls and barriers to you and not listen to what you have to say.

Ladies, when communicating with your man, ask them questions to get their perspective on things. Literally ask your man, 'What's your point of view about this? How do you see this working?' You will start to get clear on how he functions, what he wants to create in life and how you could contribute to that.

Years and years ago when I didn't work because I hated being a tiler, I would come up with different ideas for things I could do with my life. Simone, being the absolute bulldozer and creative queen that she is, would jump in with all these magnificent suggestions. She can extrapolate more from an idea in 10 minutes than most people can in a whole year. This was overwhelming for me, or so I decided at the time. That is when Gary said to her, 'You need to *not* help him unless he asks.'

When you try to help someone without being asked, they will resist it, which is what I did. So, wait and when you know you can contribute to the other person, do so from a space of invitation. The number of different things that Simone has invited me to is awesome. She always does it from a space of invitation, not from expectation.

If you really want to give your man some information, look at how you could say it in a way that he can receive it. What question could you ask? What comment could you make? What is going to work?

It might be that you have sex first, after which you have his full attention for about 10 minutes and that is the moment to get whatever you want! That is the joy and fun of manipulation in relationships and if you are willing to have that, everything would be so much easier. What if relationship was fun and not such a depressing thing that is created to fit into this reality?

MEN DON'T WANT TO TALK THINGS OUT

Simone

One of the annoying ideas about relationship, that has been perpetrated on us, is that we need to share everything with each other. Ladies, if you have been out shopping, do not come home and expect to share with your partner. That is not what he is there for. Men do not want to sit around and hear you talk about shoes. It doesn't work for them.

When I want to share something, I will find a girl-friend or a man who enjoys being a girl. Yes, they are out there!

Men don't like sharing. Men require space. There are moments in life when your partner may want to be angry or frustrated. Let him enjoy it. If Brendon is being cranky, I don't ask, 'What did I do? Is it me?' which can be frustrating to a man. I may say, 'Is there anything I can contribute?' which then gives him the choice to say yes or no.

Some men might want to sit in front of the TV for a while or read a book while they process things. I have a friend who likes to play video games. Please don't get cranky at your partner for doing things like that. If he doesn't want to talk it out, don't make him.

Chapter 16 Tools

- If you desire an easier time in relationship, communicate with your Enjoyable Other in the way they like to communicate. Are they direct or do they like to talk things out?

- When you want to give your man some information, look at how you could say it in a way that he can receive it. What question could you ask? What comment could you make? It might be that you have sex first, after which you have his full attention for about 10 minutes!

'There are moments in life when your partner may want to be angry or frustrated. Let him enjoy it.'

Simone

CHAPTER 17

What if different possibilities are available?

Simone

Something that comes up a lot with women is the necessity to hate men whether or not they have one in their life. When I hear these stories where the husband is a horrible person I often wonder why they are with these men if they are so horrible. Even if your relationship ended or you got a divorce, you don't have to get mad and angry. What if you did it from a different way instead of trauma and drama?

When I look at the men in the world, I see a kindness and a generosity of spirit to them that we have not acknowledged. At the same time there is confusion about their role.

Most of the women I know want to go out and conquer the world and so many men love taking care of everyone. What if different possibilities are available? What if women aren't meant to be at home cleaning the house, cooking and doing the laundry? What if we didn't treat each other as though a man is meant to do certain things and a woman is only meant to do certain things. What if we actually honoured each other, and asked questions of the person with whom you choose to be in relationship? Find out what makes them happy and what they would like to choose.

Years ago I used to tell my friends, 'If I ever end up with someone they will have to be okay with me saying, "Bye, honey, I am leaving. I will be back in a week or four weeks,"' because I always desired to keep travelling the world, meeting more people and changing people's lives along the way. So, if I desired to find someone, they would have to be ok with that. I remember a friend saying, 'Simone, you need a doormat.' That comment stuck with me for a time because I wondered if I was being unkind.

What I now realise is that you are being unkind to your partner if you give yourself up. You are being unkind if you are not willing to be everything you can be every single day and desire the same thing for your partner.

And, what if you could have more than one man in your life? (It is *not* what you think! Let me give you more information about this.)

There are about five men in my life who are such a contribution to me. Brendon is the one with whom I choose to live, travel and have sex. He is fun to be around and makes amazing meals. We are creating some phenomenal things together including our financial reality. We do this by continuously asking questions about what else we can add to our lives. It doesn't have to be about us doing everything together; it is about being a continuous contribution to each other.

I have another four male friends who are major contributions to my life in different ways. Some of them travel with me when Brendon is around, and also when Brendon is not around. We have a communion and a friendship that is invaluable to me.

I would never consider excluding other men from my life based on my relationship with Brendon. Yet I see people do that all the time. They think they have to be exclusively with one person. For most people, the moment they start to do exclusion in relationship, they go to a conclusion and limitation of what can be.

I am *not* saying that I go out and have sex with other men, I actually don't choose to. Every day when I ask myself who I would like to have sex with today, it is always Brendon. It is a choice for me and is not based on necessity.

I have different men in my life with whom I love having dinner or sharing a glass of wine and talking about creation. They are some of the most incredibly creative, intelligent, smart men on the planet who are involved in different areas of my life and my business and are a contribution to my growth. My willingness to receive from all of them creates more in my life and living.

Being a female, even a strong and dynamic one like myself, doesn't mean I won't allow men to treat me as a lady. One of the favourite aspects of having so many kind and generous men in my life is that they treat me like a lady. Whether it is opening a car door or holding my chair for me in a restaurant. One of them has sent me more flowers than Brendon has! It doesn't mean anything.

I didn't always find it easy to receive from people who desire to contribute to me. I remember being on a flight with a male friend, and struggling to get a bag from the overhead locker in the plane.

He said, 'Simone, do you realise if you ask me for help, I would move mountains for you?'

If you are someone who is fiercely independent it may take a level of vulnerability to ask for contribution. When you do, what shows up in their world and your world is far greater than you could ever imagine.

THE DESIRE FOR SPACE

Brendon

In order to have a conscious relationship you require three things:

1. That they contribute monetarily or in some other way like I did when I was cooking meals for Simone every night;

2. That they are good in bed;

3. That they let the other person do whatever they want.

So many relationships are based on control. It is all about he should do a, b, c and I will do x, y, z. If you are looking for just one tool that will create a greater relationship for you, then let your partner do whatever they want to, when they want to.

Some people might find that terrifying. It is actually quite liberating.

Even the simple tool of giving your partner space, which I mentioned before, will create a greater relationship for you. Occasionally, Simone or I might go and sleep downstairs in the guest room alone, just because we require space as a being.

Recognise when you require space or when your partner requires it and don't make yourself wrong. You will have a longer, happier relationship if you are willing to allow each other to have space and have choice. Giving your partner choice is one of the most valuable things you could do. You give them choice and guess what? They don't want to leave.

If someone needs space it is simply their choice and that does not mean you have done something wrong or been a bad partner in the relationship. There was one occasion when Simone wanted to have the house all to herself, just for a night. I adore Simone and I immediately looked at what I could do to create that. So Nash and I went camping. We were away for two or three days and we had a great time. In most relationships, if someone asked for space, it would be considered a problem and you now have to sit down and work things through.

JEALOUSY IS A DISTRACTION

Simone

One night not long after we got together, Brendon and I were watching a movie together and Cameron Diaz was in it. I don't remember the movie, but I do recall saying, 'Isn't she hot? Look at her legs.' Brendon just looked at me without saying anything. I discovered that in his previous relationship he could not talk about another woman without it leading to a fight. If Brendon even looked sideways at a woman, his girlfriend would accuse him of wanting to cheat on her and yell and scream at him. There were numerous times when she accused him of cheating on her even though he never did. He could not even watch a movie and look like he was lusting after another woman, because there would be World War III.

It took me quite a while to convince Brendon that I wasn't trying to trick him or trap him into anything. Jealousy is not real, it is a distraction.

Be aware that if jealousy comes up, you have the chance to destroy and uncreate it and change it in that very moment. Now that Brendon is travelling the world, there are more and more women who meet him and talk about how wonderful and handsome he is. And I am really grateful that people get to see the Brendon I see every day. I am grateful that the world gets to have him as well.

Chapter 17 Tools

- Even if you see yourself as a strong and dynamic female, be vulnerable and allow the kind and caring men in your life to treat you as a lady.

- Recognise when you require space or when your partner requires it and don't make yourself wrong.

'One tool that will create a greater relationship for you, is to let your partner do whatever they want to, when they want to.'

Brendon

CHAPTER 18

Are we done yet?

Simone

By now you will have realised that I have a different perspective. To me, relationship is about two different people who have chosen to be together for a space to create something that is far greater than each of them could create alone.

When that is the basis of staying together, it is easy to recognise if the relationship is over. This takes all the upset and angst out of breakups. Unfortunately, there is lots of research to show that people prefer to be in an unhappy relationship, than be without one. This never made much sense to me because if I was done with someone, then why would I want to stay in relationship with them? When I was younger, I had really good friendships with my ex-boyfriends. We didn't break up from trauma and drama; it was more from a sense of moving on. There was always kindness towards each other.

Ending a marriage or relationship doesn't have to be disempowering for either party. What if you bought a bottle of champagne and said, 'Hey, you know what? This was great...'

Brendon

High fives!

Simone

Yes, high fives! And, 'Have we done what we came together to do on this planet? Yes? Thank you so much. Let's move on.'

Many people stay in a relationship because they are looking for security and safety. A relationship is not secure and it is not safe. How many people were you with in the past who you are no longer in a relationship with now? So how secure was the relationship?

Most people wait until they start fighting. Or they wait for the other person to leave. It is really rare for two people to simultaneously recognise that the relationship isn't working, yet I have friends who did just that. They chose to get divorced and went through the process with such ease that it has been a contribution to them and their children. Even though there are moments when things aren't easy, they continue to support each other in creating phenomenal lives. They share the parenting and if they need to change the schedule, or tweak it, they will do so without having to fight about it. My friend says, 'Change isn't loss. Change can also be creation.'

Brendon

If you are in a relationship that is ending and you are getting divorced, you don't have to have all the usual trauma and drama even though this is what gets projected at you.

Just after I got out of a long-term relationship, a friend said to me, 'You will get over it. It will just take a couple of years.'

I bought that point of view hook, line and sinker. Funnily enough, it did take me a couple of years to get over my relationship at the time. Had I been pragmatic, I would have acknowledged that I simply didn't want to be in a relationship any longer; instead I created sadness and upset that it had ended.

It is the same with a marriage breakup. People will tell you, 'This is how it should look. You will hurt for this amount of time. You will have to go through this. This is going to happen.' When you buy someone's point of view as true and real for you, that is exactly what you will create.

Simone

If your relationship is not working for you, then look at what would have to change so that it *does* work for you. Give yourself some space, whether it is going for a walk on the beach or in the woods. Look at what eight things the other person would have to change so your relationship is based on kindness, caring, nurturing, allowance, choice and possibility.

Write those eight things down. Don't put them up on the fridge or tell your partner or demand that he or she changes to suit you! This is about *you* getting clear on the relationship you desire.

Now look at those eight things you wrote down. Can your partner deliver that? Is this actually possible, or would it be like asking a leopard to change its spots? There may be five things out of eight, or one thing, or eight out of eight that can be changed. Be brutally honest and, if six things can be changed and the other two can't, is that going to work for you? If you have kids, take them into consideration also.

I see so many people who have already decided that they must stay together unhappily for the rest of their lives. By that very conclusion they are killing their future possibilities. If you are doing that, you are creating a limited, contractive life, rather than an expansive future because in truth you could split up and get remarried in five years' time — anything could happen.

Brendon

If you have a relationship that is no longer fun, that doesn't mean you have to throw it away. People often say, 'Well, this relationship isn't working; he is not doing what I want, or she is not doing what I want, so I will throw it away.'

Every morning, take some time to destroy and un-create your relationship with your wife or girlfriend, so you begin the day with a clean slate and the least amount of baggage.

Also, ask yourself every day, 'Do I desire to be in this relationship?' If you get 'No,' that doesn't mean you must quit the relationship and leave. Ask more questions: 'What is it going to take to change this?' and 'Do I desire to change this?'

Be honest and vulnerable with yourself because a relationship is something that you create daily. If you are willing to have no expectations and no projections of each other, your relationship will get a thousand times better. Just that little piece of information will create dramatic change, because I see so many people having expectations and projections of themselves in relationship and of each other.

To give you just a small example, Simone does not expect romantic gestures from me like sending her flowers, ever. This year on Valentine's Day I was in Australia and she was in Denver, Colorado. I sent her a massive bouquet of flowers just for the fun of it. She absolutely loved it. I wasn't trying to prove anything. Yet how many people act as though they need to prove their love so the other person can be secure in the relationship? It doesn't work. If you need to prove something in your relationship, then you have already decided something is wrong.

Often times you have decided that either you are wrong or the other person is wrong, which is actually just a judgement. Judgement is one of the killers of relationship. I couldn't have a relationship with someone who judges me and makes me wrong. Simone would most probably say the same thing.

Chapter 18 Tools

- Every day ask yourself, 'Do I desire to be in this relationship?' If you get 'No,' that doesn't mean you must quit the relationship. Ask more questions: 'What is it going to take to change this?' and 'Do I desire to change this?'

- Having no expectations or projections of each other will make your relationship a thousand times better! Try it and see what shows up.

> *'Ending a marriage or relationship doesn't have to be disempowering for either party.'*
>
> Simone

CHAPTER 19

And now we begin…

Brendon

Have you ever had someone in your life to whom you wished to get closer and no matter what you did, you couldn't? You could get fairly close to them and no closer?

This is quite a common scenario in all areas of life, not only in relationships. What we do is create a comfortable distance between us and everyone else. We keep this safe distance because we have decided that otherwise we would have no sense of self or everyone would know our secrets and that would be a bad thing.

When I began facilitating Access Choice of Possibility classes around the world, I finally realised what Gary had meant when he said, 'You will not be able to have secrets anymore.' To facilitate these classes, I had to drop all of my barriers and be totally vulnerable.

This was not how I used to live my life. In the past I used distance as a way to create separation in my relationships. Either I created a comfortable distance with someone, or else they created a comfortable distance with me and we both maintained it.

It is rather like always having the back door open, so you can run away from them or get out of the relationship at any time. You never fully commit to the other person. If you never commit to another, you never commit to you and you never commit to *your* life.

Comfortable distance is not logical or linear. It is not cognitive or obvious. So if you get a sense that you have been creating a comfortable distance between you and someone or something, please start asking questions about it. The purpose of asking questions is to gain awareness so you can change whatever is going on; it is not to get an answer.

What I realised was that I had used comfortable distance so I wouldn't have to show up in the world. I would show up a little bit, yet keep most of me hidden away. I was hiding everything I am actually capable of, so that other people wouldn't judge me or think I was crazy.

Have you been keeping a comfortable distance between you and your partner, or between you and your business?

Have you created a comfortable distance between you and money? We make so many decisions about what it means to have lots of money: that we will have to give it away, or we wouldn't know what to do with it. Those are all the ways we create comfortable distance between us and the money we say we desire to have.

CHAOS AND THE ADVENTURE OF LIVING

Simone

I would like to ask you a question you may never have considered before: *What if every single moment you spend in your relationship was a choice?* It would be like going on a holiday where nothing was planned and there was no order to your day. You simply woke up every morning and choose to have fun and the adventure of living. That is what it is like when you function from chaos in your life and in your relationship.

We have misidentified chaos as a bad thing and order as a good thing. In actuality chaos will create a relationship that is always expanding, never contractive and always creating greater possibilities with every choice you make.

We have all seen relationships where everything is based on trauma and drama; screaming and shouting, mayhem and upset. That is havoc; that is not chaos.

Chaos is the creative energy of all possibilities. Chaos is question. Chaos will create a relationship that is always gifting infinite choice and infinite possibilities. Whether you are single or married; whether you think you want to be out of a relationship or in a relationship; whether you think you want to be gay or straight, instilling chaos will get you to true choice.

You do *not* have to be the same as everybody else.

The relationship that will work for you is not necessarily your parent's relationship. It is not your best friend's relationship. The relationship that works for you is the one you choose and if you are willing to instil chaos it will be greater.

It is not difficult to instil chaos. All you have to do is ask for it. Here are some examples:

- How much chaos would I have to instil to have choices beyond this reality?

- What would it be like if I instilled chaos into my relationship?

- What chaos can I instil to create sex that expands my life?

If you are willing to instil chaos you won't know what will happen next. Your relationship will no longer be ordered, automatic and predictable, which is so boring anyway.

We have been taught to live an ordered life where we do our best to fit in and try not to stand out too much. Order is trying to work everything out. For instance, have you ever had the experience of seeing someone across a crowded room and had an irresistible urge to talk to them? If you fall over yourself to get to someone, my best advice is: run. Run, because you have already started to instil the order of what your relationship must look like even before you exchange two words with them. When you order that everything has to be a certain way, you keep your relationship from changing. You limit the possibilities that can show up, because order has nothing to do with creation.

Order is about staying together 'till death do you part'. Order is planning everything in your life down to the nth degree. In sex, order is the idea that he must do this; she must do this. Or, it is Wednesday night, time for sex, rather than having sex whenever it is fun to have sex.

The order of family is usually the place where you are defined and limited, because how many families encourage you to be great? I don't see very many families that are encouraging and enthusiastic for you to be you. Usually, family wants to stick you in a box rather than encourage you to be the chaos of you.

What if chaos put the joy back in relationship? What if chaos put the joy back in sex? What if all the fun you have been hoping your life could be is embodied in the chaos that is actually your true possibility?

Chaos is not right and order is not wrong. What is required is coherence between order and chaos so you have a sense of ease and possibility with everything in life, including relationship.

CONTINUOUSLY PLAYING WITH POSSIBILITIES

Simone

The greatest gift you can give the person with whom you are in relationship is choice.

A year or two ago I got an awareness that I wanted to live in Europe for about six months. When I talked to Brendon about it he said half-jokingly, 'Yes, and will you still contribute to the mortgage?'

Brendon did not try to hold on to me or say, 'You can't go to Europe because you are in relationship with me and I have to stay in Australia.' If I desired to live in Europe he was willing for me to go.

It wasn't about us breaking up either. Or me having to choose between staying with Brendon and Nash, and going off to Europe for a few months. How often do you see people make their choices based on resistance to one another? Rather like tit for tat, 'Well you did this, so now I am going to do this.'

Every choice Brendon and I make is an honouring of ourselves and each other. In Access it is called functioning from the Kingdom of We. We look at each choice and what that will create in our relationship. I will even ask a question like, 'If I choose this, what will our relationship be like?'

I would never make a choice *against* Brendon. The Kingdom of We is how you include others around you and also choose for you. You don't eliminate yourself or what you desire, which a lot of people seem to do in relationship. You have continuous choice and vulnerability, so that you can be as great as you are and the other person can be as great as they are.

Now, I haven't gone to live in Europe yet. It has led to some different discussions about our future. We continuously play with different possibilities. We are investing in a magnificent, ancient castle in Italy that is being restored and turned into a luxurious boutique hotel. Maybe in a couple of years' time we will get a place in Spain or in the south of France. Who knows how it will show up? When you allow yourself true choice it will always create more for you and your relationship even though it may seem like you are rocking the boat.

THE DISCOMFORT OF AWARENESS

Brendon

In so many areas of life there *are* times when things get uncomfortable, yet often something much greater is just beyond it. From experience, every time I got to an uncomfortable place that in the past I would run away from, I started asking myself: what if I just stayed with this? What if I kept pushing into it? Because what makes comfortable a good thing and uncomfortable a bad thing? It is our point of view, because both good and bad are judgements.

The very first time I co-facilitated the Access Choice of Possibilities class with Gary Douglas in Mumbai, India, I was so uncomfortable I was 'sweating bullets' as the saying goes. As soon as I could, during the first break, I went straight to my room and poured myself a drink. After a while I calmed down enough to use some tools and gain more clarity. One of the questions I asked myself: *what is true for me here?* I realised that I had different choices. I could leave or I could go back to the class and be myself. I didn't have to be like Gary and I didn't have to facilitate like Gary. So after the break I went to class and was myself and everything got easier.

Whether in relationship or another area in your life, what have you decided is too uncomfortable for you to choose?

These days I am rarely comfortable. That doesn't mean I give up comfort of my body. My body likes comfort and nice clothes, good food, jet skiing etc. For me the being, I know that every time I get uncomfortable there is more beyond that. It is always greater on the other side.

I could say a million things about this, yet when you get this awareness for yourself, you will have it forever. When you get to that uncomfortable place that makes you want to turn around and run the other way, recognise that energy. What if instead of saying, 'It is too hard,' or 'I am shitting myself,' this time you were willing to do whatever it is that makes you uncomfortable?

This is all about having more choice. When there is no comfortable distance between you and everyone else, more choices are available to you. And, if you want a different relationship, you have to choose something different. You can't do the same thing every day, or make a small change and expect your whole life to be different. You literally must make different choices — and it doesn't have to be hard.

THERE IS NO SUCH THING AS THE ONE

Simone

You don't have to be lucky in love. There is a difference to creating a relationship based on what you desire, not what you need and require. What is your choice with relationship? Every single person has something different that they would like to create in life. Of course, whatever you desire has to work for the person you are choosing to be in relationship with. As an example, my desire is to travel around the world and to facilitate Access Consciousness classes. I travel between nine and ten months out of each year. Sometimes I travel with Brendon and sometimes I travel alone. My desire and demand to have the tools of Access out in the world and to have more consciousness on this planet is a huge priority of mine. If Brendon was someone who said, 'No, I need you to be at home, looking after our child or doing the cooking and laundry,' then our relationship wouldn't work.

The disparity of what you desire has to create the disparate relationship you have. It may not be congruent with this reality. How many people create relationship as a completion — it is the box they live in. They choose to have kids, get married, buy a house, get a dog and that is it. Then they start to maintain the conclusion they have created rather than continuously creating the relationship. Another thing that occurs for many people is they create a relationship that is congruent to the projections of what society tells you that relationship should be.

Aren't you supposed to be happy once you find The One and get married? Guess what? There is no such thing as The One! I remember years and years ago overhearing my mother talk to someone about me and say, 'Oh, she will be happy when she finds The One.' Seriously! I was already one of the happiest people I knew.

Yet how many people judge that happiness means finding The One, marriage, kids, a dog and a house with a picket fence? Now, you can have that as a choice, you don't need to resist that, but it doesn't equal happiness. You, waking up in the morning and choosing to be happy is what creates happiness. What if you were willing to create your relationship so that it is in constant creation? That is total disparity with how relationship is done in this reality.

Love is not about luck. Love actually stands for Lower Oscillating Vibrating Equivalence. So many people create this place where they are highly creative, not in need and then they meet someone whom they think is awesome. Then, they decide they better oscillate to the other person's vibration. What if you could have two people in relationship who are in constant creation yet they didn't have to be congruent with each other? Quite often, Brendon and I are on opposite sides of the world. We are still in communion with each other. We still empower each other to choose everything that the other person would possibly desire to choose and more.

It is a constant place of gratitude and being the five elements of intimacy.

Brendon

We called this book, *Relationship: are you sure you want one?* so that people will look at what it is they desire to create in life. Not everyone wants a relationship; it is not a given. If *you* desire a phenomenal relationship, start choosing and use all the tools we have talked about here.

Creation begins with choices. How often do you hear someone say, 'I can't believe this happened to me?' I have said it myself. Nothing ever happens to you, you create it from the choices you make. Everything that has shown up in your life is the result of your choices.

One thing you have to get is there is nothing wrong with you and there is no such thing as a wrong choice. I could say that I make wrong choices all the time, and yet they are not wrong choices because they give me awareness. Oftentimes things don't work out the way I have decided that they should! That doesn't make my choice wrong. I recognise, 'Wow, that didn't work, now what can I choose?' Every time you choose you will get awareness of the direction in which you would like your life to go.

*So now, who am I going
to choose to BE?*

Gender translator

For those of you who are interested in communicating with the other sex, here is a translating system you might find useful!

WOMEN'S ENGLISH

Yes = No

No = Yes

Maybe = No

We need = I want

I am sorry = You'll be sorry

We need to talk = You're dead meat

Sure, go ahead = If you do it you will pay

Do what you want = You will pay dearly for this later

We are going to do this = You are going to do this!

I am not upset = Of course I am upset you moron!

You are certainly attentive today = Is sex all you ever think about?

MEN'S ENGLISH

I am hungry = I am hungry

I am sleepy = I am sleepy

I am tired = I am tired

Nice dress = Nice cleavage!

I love you = Let's have sex now

I am bored = Would you like to have sex?

May I have this dance? = I'd like to have sex with you!

Do you want to go to the movies? = Would you like to have sex with me?

Can I take you out for dinner? = Can we have sex now?

I don't think those shoes go with that outfit = I'm gay

This excerpt is from the Access Consciousness®, Choice of Possibilities class manual.

About Simone Milasas

Simone Milasas is a lady who knows how to be a woman, who sees the joy of possibility and future and knows that there is the prospect of possibility in every choice you choose.

Simone has worked in many different industries around the world. She has owned companies, created them, managed them, changed them all with an enthusiasm to invite people to a different possibility in the world.

"I grew up with the question of 'Imagine what you would do if you knew you could not fail?' – to me you cannot fail, failure is just the start of something new" says Simone.

Simone has always believed that anything is possible and desired to inspire people to choose everything they could.

"True leadership is knowing where you are heading and not allowing anyone to stop you. You have to know what you wish to create." Simone is the worldwide coordinator of Access Consciousness, a forever expanding company in over 176 countries.

Simone is the author of JOY OF BUSINESS translated into 13 languages and best-selling book GETTING OUT OF DEBT JOYFULLY translated into 5 languages. She is currently working on her 3rd book with Brendon Watt called; Relationship. Are you sure you want one?

Simone currently travels the world facilitating seminars with Access Consciousness. She also has numerable online courses and is always asking for more possibilities to show up. You can find Simone every week on her podcast – The Art & Industry of Business & Living available on her website www.simonemilasas.com and iTunes.

About Brendon Watt

Brendon Watt is a speaker, entrepreneur, business and life mentor. He is the Australian CFO of Access Consciousness®, a set of simple-yet-profound tools currently transforming lives in 176 countries, and the facilitator of several special Access programs including Access Bars®, Conscious Parenting Conscious Kids, and Joy of Business.

Growing up, Brendon always recognised the 'difference' in him, yet he spent all his time trying to fit in and be the same as everyone else. After decades of conformity, he was struggling for money and living in a tiny room in his mother's home with his four-year-old child. When he discovered the pragmatic tools of Access Consciousness®, Brendon made the choice to change his life for the better. Today he is in a happy relationship, with a healthy investment portfolio, and travels regularly – sharing and facilitating the tools that changed his reality and empowering others to know that anything is possible.

Drawing upon his transformation from a struggling tradesman and single dad to global speaker and CFO, Brendon facilitates classes and workshops all over the world, empowering others to know they are not wrong, that anything is possible and that they are only one choice away from change. Find more at www.brendonwatt.com

For more on *Relationship — Are You Sure You Want One?*

There is more possible! Explore Brendon and Simone's online course on Kajabi, get new relationship tools delivered to your inbox and create a Relationship Done Different at

www.relationshipareyousureyouwantone.com

Relationship Done Different classes are offered around the world. Find a class near you

www.relationshipsdonedifferent.com

Lightning Source UK Ltd.
Milton Keynes UK
UKHW040614230219
337623UK00001B/3/P